PATCHWORK, PLEASE!

colorful Zakka projects to stitch *AND* give

Ayumi Takahashi

INTERWEAVE
interweave.com

EDITOR Marlene Blessing
TECHNICAL EDITOR Katrina Walker
ART DIRECTOR Liz Quan
DESIGNER Julia Boyles
ILLUSTRATOR Missy Shepler
PHOTOGRAPHER Joe Hancock
PHOTO STYLIST Pamela Chavez
PRODUCTION DESIGNER Katherine Jackson

Interweave Press LLC,
a division of F+W Media Inc.
201 East Fourth Street
Loveland, CO 80537
interweave.com

Printed in China by Asia Pacific Offset Ltd.

Library of Congress
Cataloging-in-Publication Data

Takahashi, Ayumi.
Patchwork, please! : colorful zakka projects
to stitch and give / Ayumi Takahashi.
    pages cm
Includes bibliographical references and index.
 ISBN 978-1-59668-599-4 (pbk.)
1. Textile crafts--Japan. 2. Patchwork--
Patterns. I. Title.
TT715.T35 2013
 746.46--dc23
                        2012032362

10 9 8 7 6 5 4 3 2 1

acknowledgments

A big, big hug for everyone at
Interweave! I especially thank
Tricia Waddell and Allison
Korleski for encouraging me to
write this book, and for having
been constantly supportive
of me. I also thank Marlene
Blessing and Katrina Walker for
editing my book very beautifully,
and Elaine Lipson for giving me
great insights. I thank all the
people I have met in the online
craft community who have
inspired me to sew and keep
creating without fear. Thank
you to my grandma, mom,
and mother-in-law, Kim, for
inspiring me to start my sewing
adventure. Last but not least,
I deeply thank my husband, Joe,
for always being there for me,
for being proud of my projects,
and for putting up with the noisy
sewing machine in our small
apartment.

Contents

for the kitchen

for kids

for the home

for going places

for crafting

Introduction

Born into a family that treasures the process of crafting, I naturally became interested in sewing. My grandma, who spent fifty years of her life working in the clothing industry, sewed lots of clothes for me as I grew up. Whenever I had an idea of something she could make for me, I would ask my mom to stop by a fabric store on the way to grandma's house. My heart would pound with excitement every time I was in front of shelves packed with beautiful fabric bolts, as I imagined the possibilities each fabric held. Dresses? Bags? Baby shoes? Dreaming about transforming fabric into something useful got me really excited. My mom, who majored in sewing in school, was a great inspiration, too. I grew up watching her sew for my sisters and me and, at times, for a craft bazaar. I saw my grandma and mother as superwomen, because they knew how to use that loud gigantic thing that somehow produces lovely things: a sewing machine!

I can't think of anybody who is more passionate about creating and designing, especially for other people, than my dad. As an architect, he has designed many houses in Japan. When he designed a house for our family, he was nice enough to include me, a ten-year-old, in the design process. I chose wallpaper for the bathroom from a thick catalog. I picked the most animated, crazy one (rows of serious-looking cat faces), which still makes people laugh when they visit the house. Whether or not it was a good choice of wallpaper, my dad surely succeeded in teaching me about the joy of design.

It wasn't until I was an adult that I first dipped my toes into a serious sewing adventure. When I spent my first Christmas with my husband Joe's (back then boyfriend) family in Yakima, Washington, I saw lovely Christmas stockings hung on the wall. They were all different, custom made by my mother-in-

law, Kim, with each person in mind. I was absolutely touched to see my Christmas stocking hanging next to everyone else's. I felt so warm and fuzzy—almost teary. That was when I rediscovered my love of handmade. I knew I wanted to sew and to be able to transfer the love of handmade items through gift-giving.

I was lucky enough to live close to a great fabric store with a lot of modern fabrics. Even though I didn't yet have a sewing machine, I began collecting fabrics from that store. Whenever I needed a little lift during the day, I would stop by the store and pick up a few fat quarters to pet and adore. (I used to call it *fabric therapy*.) Joe surprised me in the summer of 2006 by gifting me the best thing ever: a sewing machine! Ever since, I have never lived without sewing.

In April 2008, after teaching myself how to sew small *zakka* items,

I started my sewing blog, Pink Penguin (ayumills.blogspot .com) in order to become a part of the growing online craft community. (*Zakka,* which translates to "many things," refers to objects that improve your home, life, or appearance.) Being a part of the blogging community has brought me to a higher level in my sewing journey. It has been completely amazing to make friends online who share the joy of playing with fabrics.

Over time, I've discovered that patchwork is the most satisfying form of sewing art for me. I enjoy never knowing how a finished patchwork project will look until I complete it. I can come up with my very own designs using fabrics I love. Quite often, several different fabrics will unexpectedly come together and create uniform, beautiful work of art. Such a transformation is a joy to see. I find patchwork versatile and eco-friendly too: if you don't like the way your patchwork turned out, just rip out the seams and try a different fabric combination. (Learning to be good friends with your seam ripper is one way to enjoy patchwork projects more!) Keep in mind that any leftover fabric scraps from projects have lots of potential, so don't throw them away.

I hope the projects in this book will inspire you to sew something. All the projects are suitable for anybody with basic sewing experience. Even if you are new to sewing, don't worry; this book has all the information you'll need to get started, from a list of materials to techniques described in detail. With a beginning sewist in mind, I have avoided difficult techniques such as needle-turn appliqués and Y-shaped seams. My goal is to inspire anyone to enjoy sewing, especially with small scraps.

I always try to remind myself that learning to sew through trial and error (many errors for me!) is a natural process. Sewing won't be as fun and pleasing if everything you make comes out perfectly every time. It is okay to produce things you aren't the most proud of every once in a while, because you definitely learn something each time you create that will help make better projects later. The more sewing projects you work on, the more you'll realize what makes you happy, what kinds of fabric combinations and colors you find most lovely. Soon you will have your own distinctive patchwork style!

Tools & Materials

In this chapter, you'll find the tools and materials you'll need to make each project in this book and beyond. Having the right tools and materials is the key to enjoying pleasant crafting times and satisfying results. Everything listed here can be found at your local craft stores, as well as from online sources. Good-quality tools last longer, and often provide the very best results. Although they are pricey, I recommend you get the highest-quality tools you can afford.

basic quilting tools

SEWING MACHINE

There are so many different types of sewing machines available. To make the projects in this book, your sewing machine should have these three basic functions: an adjustable stitch length, a straight stitch, and a zigzag stitch. Everything in this book was made using a standard, nothing-fancy Janome DC4030. I recommend buying your first sewing machine from a local sewing machine store. The staff will likely be knowledgeable and will let you try out the machine so that you'll have a chance to see if it will fit your needs. Be sure to ask any questions you may have so you will be satisfied you have chosen the right machine for you. Many sewing machine stores provide free regular maintenance service, and often sewing classes, too. As your sewing machine will need maintenance at least once a year, it is great to have a familiar, trusted place where you can take your machine when it needs maintenance/repair. Your sewing machine's manual should have a tutorial on cleaning and oiling your machine regularly on your own. You might be surprised to see the huge lint balls that form from the fibers of fabrics and threads that become embedded in your machine! Regular cleaning and oiling will keep your machine running smoothly and help avoid repairs.

SPECIALIZED SEWING-MACHINE PRESSER FEET

In addition to the regular presser foot that comes with your sewing machine, you'll need a zipper foot and a walking foot for quilting. I also highly recommend a ¼" (6 mm) foot, which helps you achieve a consistent ¼" (6 mm) seam allowance. Slippery fabrics such as laminated or vinyl-coated fabric tend to stick and grip rather than feed evenly under the presser foot: I recommend a Teflon-coated sewing-machine foot to eliminate this problem. Alternatively, you can use tracing paper on top of and underneath your project. (After stitching, the tracing paper is removed.)

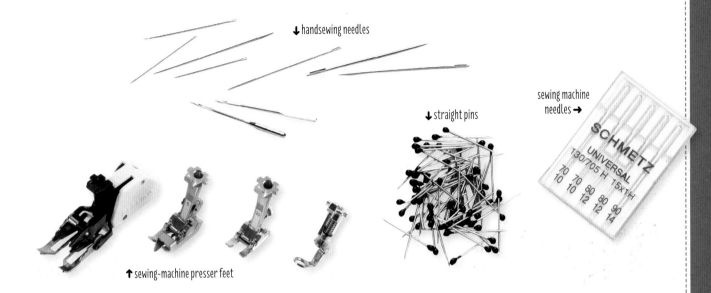

↓ handsewing needles

↓ straight pins

sewing machine
needles →

↑ sewing-machine presser feet

SEWING-MACHINE NEEDLES

Your sewing-machine needles should be matched to the weight of your fabric. A lot of problems are often caused by using needles that aren't well suited to the fabric. The heavier your fabric is, the thicker your needle should be. For all the projects in this book, a regular point Universal needle (size 80/12) for woven fabrics is appropriate.

IRON AND IRONING BOARD

Ironing your fabric before you begin is very important for achieving smooth piecing. It is definitely worth investing in a high-quality iron. I use an Oliso iron that has an automatic feature for elevating itself when not in use. This means that I never have to turn my wrist to let the iron stand on its end. Previously, I had a cheap iron that got too hot when it sat 'on' for a while, which often scorched my fabric—no fun. My Oliso iron never gets too hot and has never burned my fabric. I love it to bits!

The larger the ironing board is, the easier the ironing process will be, especially if you are working on larger projects. If you like to work small, I recommend having a Clover mini-iron and a small ironing board that you can place on your work table next to your sewing machine. Never having to stand up to iron is quite nice!

STRAIGHT PINS

Pins hold two or more layers of fabric together and also hold sewing patterns in place on fabric. The more pins you use, the more accurate your stitching is. I use glass head pins and flat head pins. The thicker pins are stronger, but create larger holes. For fabric that is a heavier weight, I use thick pins; the holes disappear if I stroke the parted threads a little. For lighter weight fabric, I like to use thinner pins so that the holes aren't as obvious after the pins are removed.

HANDSEWING NEEDLES

You will need two types of needles to make projects in this book—sharps and embroidery needles. General-purpose sewing needles are called sharps. These are used to close up openings by handstitching, etc. Embroidery needles have a large eye for flosses to pass through. If you would like to handquilt your projects, you'll also need quilting needles to pass through layers of your quilted projects smoothly. These are smaller and thinner than both sharps and embroidery needles.

MARKING TOOLS

My favorite marking tool is a Clover mechanical pencil, which comes with an assortment of colored leads. I like this pencil because there is no need to sharpen its tip. A water-soluble fabric marking pen is a great tool, too, as the ink disappears like magic when you dab a little bit of water on the marks.

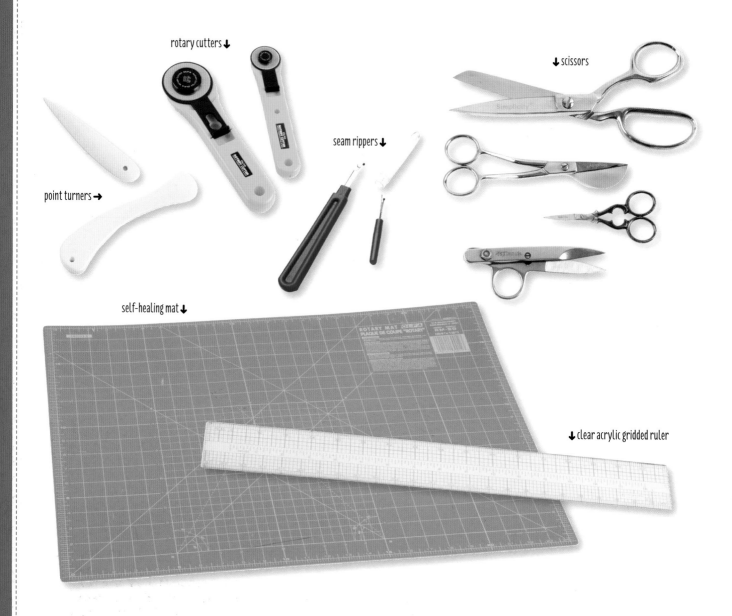

rotary cutters ↓

↓ scissors

point turners →

seam rippers ↓

self-healing mat ↓

↓ clear acrylic gridded ruler

ROTARY CUTTER

A 45 mm Olfa rotary cutter is great! Remember to replace your blade once it dulls. The first sign of dullness is when you cut fabric and some threads in the fabric remain uncut.

It's nice to have one extra rotary cutter with a dull blade for cutting paper. I've found that a dull blade can still work very nicely for this purpose.

SELF-HEALING MAT

When you cut fabrics using a rotary cutter, you will need this mat as a cutting surface. It comes in many sizes and is readily available at craft stores. This mat's surface has a grid that is useful for measuring and cutting fabrics. Buy as large a mat as you have space for. It lasts a long time, so get one you really like! (I have one with a pink surface on one side and yellow on the other.)

CLEAR ACRYLIC GRIDDED RULERS

Rulers come in various shapes and sizes. I recommend rulers with a minimum of ⅛" (3 mm) grids. It is helpful to have several different rulers so you can choose one appropriate for the scale of your project. Small square ones (up to 8" [20.5 cm] at one edge) are useful for small projects, whereas long ones (up to 23" [58.5 cm] long) are useful for cutting yardage.

SCISSORS

I don't know if it's just me, but I keep losing scissors under the layers of material while cutting multiple fabrics, so I like to have a few in each size: large scissors (8"–9" [20.5–23 cm] long) to cut fabrics, small scissors (3"–5" [7.5–12.5 cm] long) to cut thread, and pinking shears.

SEAM RIPPER

A must have! This is used to remove unwanted threads from your projects, to carefully undo sewn seams that aren't straight or have other problems, and to open buttonholes easily. I've had some good times with my ripper. Even my husband has mastered using it, since he has helped me rip out seams many times!

POINT TURNER

This is used to create neat-looking corners (such as bottom corners of a bag). I often use a chopstick for this. I like that its pointy end is not too sharp, and that it's the perfect length for most of my projects. Commercial point turners are either made of wood or plastic.

materials

FABRIC

I know I am not the only one who is completely addicted to fabric shopping, and is constantly having a problem finding space to store more fabrics! It's so much fun to collect fabric and build your stash. It's as if you are creating a little fabric shop inside your home, but this fabric store carries only fabrics you covet

{ **tip** }

Fabrics that are one color without any pattern or design are called solids. Well-known brands such as Kona have a wide variety of colors available and good distribution, so they are easy to find at local and online stores. Since solids do not come with information printed on the selvedge, it is easy to lose track of where you purchased them and what the color names are. It is useful to keep a file with a small swatch of each solid in your stash with identifying information (manufacturer, color name, and place you purchased it) in case you need more. This will save you time when you are searching for specific solids. If you often use solids in your patchwork, it might be worth buying a catalog of swatch samples (known as a color card) from a particular manufacturer. These are not only helpful, they are pretty, too!

and you are the only customer–woo-hoo!

The three main types of fabrics used in this book are 100-percent cotton, 100-percent linen, and cotton/linen blends. Pure cotton is great for patchwork projects and usually comes in 44" (112 cm) widths. It is easy to work with and has minimal shrinkage when washed. It comes in many different colors, patterns, and weights. Quilting-weight cotton fabric is most common, and is very easy to work with. It wrinkles easily, so iron it well before using. Linen comes in many colors and several different weights, but it is usually heavier than 100-percent cotton. It is much loved in Japan

for its durable beauty and a natural color that works well with colorful cotton and vintage prints. You can also work with dyed linens. Linen shrinks a lot in the wash, so when making washable projects, be sure to prewash your linen a couple of times, as you would launder clothing. You'll probably find that linen will be softer and a little "fluffy" after prewashing (it has a texture that is pleasing and neither smooth nor wrinkly), which looks prettier for projects like the kitchen towels (page 34) in this book. Cotton/linen-blend fabric is amazing. It is easy to deal with, like cotton, but has the body and the nice natural feel of linen. It is usually heavier than 100-percent

↑ Small scraps, big impact. My Scrappy Box, page 76

↑ A pleasing mix of teal, brown, and yellow fabrics. Books-for-Baby Quilt, page 68

↑ Cute vintage images framed by solids and overall prints.
Sweet Trips Embroidery Pouch, page 132

↑ Soft pastels. Swedish Bloom-Time Lap Quilt, page 118

cotton and can be treated just like you treat linen. Since I work with small pieces of many different fabrics, I have a shelf packed with small cuts (fat quarters, 18" × 22" [45.5 cm × 56 cm], to half yards, 18" × 44" [45.5 cm × 112 cm]), sorted by color and fiber content. Larger pieces of fabric are stored in a cabinet in the closet.

BATTING

Several patchwork projects in this book require batting. It is used between your quilt top and backing to add loft and weight. I like low-loft batts because they provide minimal thickness and keep the patchwork top nice, even after quilting. Cotton batting (as opposed to a polyester blend) is my favorite option for quilts. I use a thicker batting, such as fleece, for any project that needs more stability, such as the box pouches in this book (page 76). For projects such as hexagon trivets (page 96), the batting needs to be heat-resistant as well. Insul-bright batting is readily available at craft stores. When it's on sale, I often buy a lot, unlike printed cotton, small scraps of batting tend to be useless, and I want remnants to be large enough for future projects.

I have limited space in my small apartment in Tokyo, so I can't buy more than 3 yd (274.5 cm) of batting at a time, but if I had extra space for storage, I would buy batting on the bolt.

THREADS

All projects in this book can be made using general-purpose threads, which can be cotton or polyester. I use 100-percent polyester Gutermann sewing-machine thread, mainly because it comes in a wide range of colors and has a perfect strength for patchwork projects. It is nice to collect threads from a single brand, as your thread rack looks prettier and more organized, and you will not make the mistake of buying the wrong type of thread.

INTERFACING

Interfacing is a shaping essential when sewing patchwork projects. It makes fabric stiffer and adds a bit more body. Interfacing is available in a wide variety of weights and fiber types (woven and nonwoven) and can be found in your fabric store on the bolt or in small packages. I prefer to buy from bolts because I can touch and feel the stiffness and thickness before purchase, making it easier for me to decide how much to buy. Some interfacings are fusible on just one side, some are fusible on both sides, and others are not fusible at all. Follow the manufacturer's instructions carefully to fuse interfacing to your fabric using your iron (fusible interfacing is heat-fused). Pressing rather than ironing (moving the iron around) creates fewer

air bubbles between the fabric and interfacing. I also spray water onto a press cloth (a dishtowel works!) that I place on the interfacing before ironing to create a better seal between the interfacing and the fabric.

FUSIBLE WEB

Some projects in this book feature raw-edged appliqué, for which you'll need fusible web. Applying a hot iron to the web, which is sandwiched between two fabrics, adheres the fabrics together. Fusible web helps reduce fraying and stabilizes the appliqué as well. I recommend lightweight fusible web because thicker ones, such as Heat N Bond, are too stiff and difficult to sew on. Lightweight fusible adheres fabrics very well.

Materials for paper-piecing methods are described in detail in Techniques, on page 19.

Techniques

I love patchwork so much because of the beautiful harmony different fabrics create when they are sewn together into one project. It's absolutely thrilling to put together fabrics that make you happy, and to see the effect of each fabric in the finished patchwork result. Patchwork is addictive not only because it's pleasing, but also because we feel rewarded by the thinking process we go through before we sew fabric pieces together.

combining fabrics

For a project that uses several different kinds of printed fabrics, I sometimes find myself spending a day just going through my fabric stash to think and rethink my fabric choices. The more kinds of fabrics to be used for a single project, the more time I spend brainstorming.

This thinking time becomes more rewarding when the finished project turns out great. If you are a beginner at patchwork, I suggest you start by using fabrics from one manufacturer's fabric collection. Fabric designers do a great job designing fabrics using a consistent color palette in a collection. This basically guarantees that when those fabrics are put together, they will look lovely.

If you like a bit more challenge, go ahead and pick up whatever fabrics catch your eye at the fabric stores. If you like a scrappy, energetic look, you will probably love how those fabrics come together in a patchwork project. I have found that I really like the feel of a combination of typography fabric and retro prints. When these types of prints are combined, a great mix of modern and vintage styles results, which I love! When I mix many fabric prints, I like to focus on using only a few colors (black text

on white background, red polka dots on pink background, etc.); the fewer colors are used in each fabric, the easier it is to create a more unified (not too busy) patchwork result.

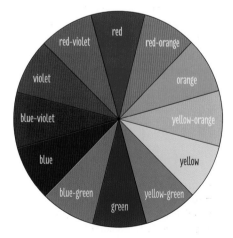

fig. 1 Keep a color wheel in your sewing room.

combining colors

Colors are completely up to you! In the patchwork world, there are no strict rules. Instead, you have the freedom to mix and match as you wish. The goal is for you to find color combinations that make you smile. One of the great ways to search for a nice color combination is to study colors in your favorite product packaging, art, or maybe just the graphics in a magazine ad. Choosing colors based on such inspirations helps us discover the color combinations we like and determine what colors of fabrics to buy for our projects. Maybe you like many colors together in a project—or you want to stick with just a few colors. As you introduce more and more colors to a project, the finished result becomes more vivid, busy, and eclectic. When you use just a few colors in a project, it creates a more serene feel.

If you want to create a project with strong contrast, pick a color from the color wheel (**fig. 1**) and choose another one from the opposite side of the wheel. For example, green is located almost 180 degrees from red, so these will create strong contrast when they are together. The closer to each other colors are on the wheel, the more they create a soft, blended feeling when they are combined. Yellow with orange, for instance, offers a calm, warm effect. In general, colors in patchwork combine beautifully if we use fabrics in a foundation palette that repeats throughout.

Pick out your first print fabric for your patchwork project, then look for a color in it that is used only slightly. Choose a next fabric that uses this color primarily. (This is easier to do if you are selecting fabrics from a single collection.) Next, lay those prints together to decide which color you want to see more of among all the existing colors in the two prints—this will be the color of the third fabric. You may feel that, instead, you want to introduce a new color. To do this, pick out a fabric with the color you think is missing so far. Keep going until you are happy with a set of colors in your fabric stash for a project. Some Web sites will help you discover nice color combinations: Design Seeds (design-seeds.com) and Color Scheme Designer (colorschemedesigner.com) are great options.

preparing fabrics

Most nonsynthetic fabrics shrink a little after being machine-washed and machine-dried. The level of shrinkage varies depending on the fabric: some 100-percent linen can shrink up to 20 percent! When you are making something that is to be washed, such as linen towels or any garment, it is important to prewash all the fabrics for the project so that major fabric shrinkage is already done before you begin your project. Machine-wash and machine-dry fabrics just as you would for the finished projects. For projects that will not be laundered, such as pincushions and pen cases, prewashing fabric is optional. Many seamstresses prewash all their fabrics regardless of the project, because they enjoy the soft feel of the fabric after its first laundering. What you'll definitely want to do for all the fabrics before cutting is spray them with water and iron them to press. While straightening up fabrics, make sure that you keep the grain of the fabric straight. This will be very helpful when you rotary-cut.

cutting fabrics

ROTARY CUTTER

To cut a straight line in a piece of fabric, I always use a rotary cutter and an acrylic ruler. It saves a lot of time and makes it much easier to achieve perfect cutting results. Holding an acrylic ruler on top of the fabric so that it doesn't shift requires a lot of strength. If you can't hold the ruler firmly enough, it will easily slip as you use a rotary cutter along the edge of the ruler. To prevent this, I use The Original Gypsy Gripper attached to my ruler (**fig. 2**). I find this helps to stabilize the ruler (you still need to apply a lot of pressure, though). I also like using this gripper for safety purposes. I haven't accidentally cut my fingernails since I started using it!

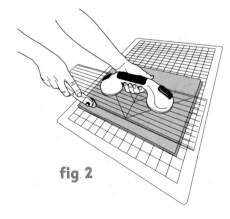

fig. 2

Before you begin cutting your fabric, make sure that the edge of the fabric you are cutting from is straight. You will need to "true up" the fabric. This is the process of ensuring that the edge of your fabric is perpendicular to the selvedges, the tightly woven edges of the fabric.

1 Fold the fabric in half with the wrong sides together, so that the selvedges of the fabric match up at the top edge. (It's exactly the way cotton fabric is folded when on the bolt.)

2 Place the folded fabric on a self-healing mat, with its folded edge facing you as a bottom edge.

3 Place the ruler on the fabric perpendicular to the fold. Cut along the edge of the ruler. You can use a gridline on the self-healing mat to ensure that the fold is placed along a horizontal line on the mat; then, place the ruler perpendicular to that fold, which is parallel to a vertical gridline from top to bottom on the self-healing mat.

4 Once the ruler is perfectly perpendicular to the fold of the fabric, you are ready to make the first cuts for your patchwork projects.

SCISSORS

Some projects in this book require templates with curvy lines. For such templates, scissors are used to cut out any shapes other than squares and triangles. (It is very hard to control a rotary cutter with a curvy line.)

pinning

The more pins you use, the easier it is to achieve a perfect result! It's as simple as that. I can't begin to tell you how many times I just rushed into finishing my projects, sewed layers together without pinning, and then said, "Oops!" Layers that were supposed to be lined up were completely off. So I had to use a seam ripper, spending a lot of time removing all the stitches to start over! I've learned that pinning is quite essential for patchwork projects, especially if I am using fabrics such as 100-percent linen, which isn't easy to control.

I like to place pins approximately 1½" (3.8 cm) apart, starting with pinning intersecting seams if there are any. Pinning close to the ends of the edge of the fabric is important, too. When there are intersecting seams, try your best to have one seam pressed to the opposite side of the corresponding seam. This will make it easier to match up the seams and to reduce bulkiness in the finished projects. This process, however, is often not easy to do when you are sewing with paper-pieced fabric because its seams are more complicated. Don't worry too much about seams when you are working on paper-piecing projects.

machine-stitching

I used my sewing machine to sew all the projects in this book. Although I have been much inspired by folks who do all sewing by hand, I've always loved sewing almost everything by machine. It's just a matter of personal preference.

STITCH LENGTH

My Janome sewing machine's normal setting for stitch length is 2.2 mm, and this is the stitch length I use for most of my projects. As I explain later in the paper-piecing section (see page 19), I prefer a shorter stitch length (1.5–1.8 mm) when I paper-piece because shorter stitches don't pull out when paper is removed. Also, some paper-piecing projects have very short edges sewn together (for example, the pencil tip on the pencil pouch on page 114.) Moreover, shorter stitches secure two layers together better; however, I would not recommend any stitch length shorter than 1.5 mm. When stitches are too short, the fabric can catch in the needle hole of the sewing machine's throat plate, making it very hard to remove the stitching when needed. I use a 2.8–3.5 mm stitch for quilting (with a walking foot). When I use my machine to baste layers of fabric, I use a long stitch length, 4–4.5 mm to make removing the thread very easy.

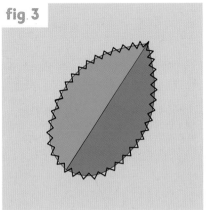

fig. 3

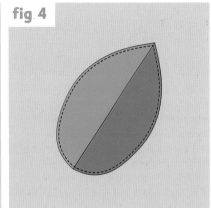

fig. 4

ZIGZAG STITCHING

Most basic sewing machines have a zigzag stitching option. I just love zigzag stitching because it looks so cute and it's hard to go wrong with it! Even if your stitching isn't straight, this will not be very noticeable, and can even appear to have been done deliberately to add a playful touch. I usually use this decorative stitching for my raw-edged appliqué (fig. 3). I change the setting of the stitch length/width based on the project. The shorter the stitch length/width is, the more secure the stitching is and the longer it takes to sew. I use short stitches for small projects/appliqués. Long zigzag stitching is great for sewing binding tapes because it has give and won't pucker. When you use the zigzag stitch setting on your machine, make sure that the machine needle penetrates the fabric in the middle position as you sew. When securing the edges of an appliqué, you want to have the edge right in the middle of the zigzag stitch so it overlaps the edge nicely. Don't worry too much about making the zigzag stitching completely straight: it can wiggle a bit at times. Only you will notice.

TOPSTITCHING

Several projects in this book have topstitched edges. This simple straight stitching adds a decorative touch to the edge of your finished project (fig. 4). To make topstitching pretty, make sure to fold over and press the edge well so that it is very flat when you stitch. If the edge is hard to press, then use many pins to secure the fold. Topstitching should be done with a normal straight-stitch length.

SEAM ALLOWANCE

This refers to the width between the edge of the fabric and the stitching that parallels it. For patchwork projects, we usually use a ¼" (6 mm) seam allowance. To make your seam allowance exactly ¼" (6 mm), you can use a fabric marker and a ruler to draw a stitching line on the fabric. However, this can be a bit too time-consuming, especially if your project is large. My favorite way to keep my seam at ¼" (6 mm) is to use a ¼" (6 mm) seam presser foot. With this foot, you simply place the edge of the fabric against the right edge of the aligning tool as you sew. If your sewing machine did not come equipped with this specialized presser foot, you can purchase one from your sewing machine's brand or try a universal one, usually available at large craft stores and/or online sources. For projects that require a larger seam allowance, I use a magnetic seam guide on my machine. This is a magnet that attaches firmly to the metal throat plate on the sewing machine. To set a magnetic guide, use a piece of fabric scrap whose width matches your desired seam allowance. With your sewing machine's needle down and the presser foot up, place the fabric against the needle on its right side. Place a magnetic seam guide so that its aligning tool abuts the fabric scrap's right edge. Remove the scrap. Now you can sew your project with its edge aligned to the magnetic guide tool, and your seam allowance will be consistent throughout.

NEEDLE TENSION ADJUSTMENT

Ideally, you want to see only the needle thread on the quilt top and the bobbin thread on the quilt back, with all stitches spaced evenly. Test a quilt sandwich sample to see how your stitching appears on both sides. If needle thread tension is too tight, the bobbin thread will appear on the quilt top. This isn't very pretty, especially if the bobbin thread is a different color from the needle thread. If this is the case, the tension needs to be lowered. On the other hand, if you see the needle threads loop on the quilt back, the needle tension needs to be tightened. (Refer to your sewing machine's instructions on how to adjust needle tension.)

handstitching

Although handstitching is time consuming, there aren't very many projects you can finish without handstitching. If you make a bag with a lining, for example, you have an opening in the lining that needs to be handsewn closed. If you make a pincushion, after stuffing it with polyester fill, you will handstitch the opening closed. Handstitching can be very relaxing and fun once you get the hang of it. I like handstitching techniques that are almost invisible. The following are the only two handstitching techniques you'll need to know to make projects in this book.

LADDER STITCHING

This is a technique for sewing two folded edges together. Your threaded needle passes through one folded edge to the other folded edge, creating a "ladder" between them. In the finished project, your stitching will be invisible (fig. 5).

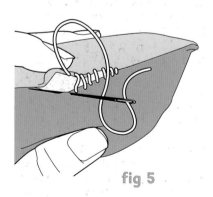

fig. 5

HANDSTITCHING TO ATTACH A BINDING TAPE

For all the projects in this book, the first stitching used to sew a binding tape on the fabric edge (one long edge sewn on the right side of the project) is done by machine. I alternated the stitching method (whether it is by hand or machine) on the other side of the long edge on the back of the project, based on the nature of the project and time constraints. For any quilted projects, I try my best to go with handstitching on the other side.

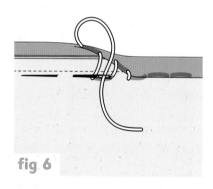

fig. 6

I like the look of a binding that is finished by handstitching much more than one done by machine sewing. It creates a very smooth and clean finish, as the stitching on the binding is invisible when handsewn (fig. 6). Since it takes a lot of time to handstitch the binding for large projects, I usually opt to machine-stitch these, using a free-motion quilting/darning foot. (The larger the project is, the less one notices small details such as handstitching on binding!) The technique for handstitching binding on the back of quilted projects is very similar to ladder stitching. You are sewing as if you are creating a ladder that connects the fold of

the binding to the main project. Handstitching is only recommended when the project has several layers. When you are binding a single layer of fabric (for example, a kitchen towel), I highly recommend machine-stitching, as your handstitching will not be invisible when there is only a single layer of fabric to hide the stitches.

quilting

Quilting is a method for sewing three layers together: a quilt top, batting, and a quilt backing. It can be done either by hand or machine. For a professional result, you can have your local quilt shop or a long-arm quilter (someone who has a long-arm sewing machine at home and provides quilting services) quilt for you. I have machine-stitched all the quilted projects in this book, since most are not too large or time-consuming. I occasionally adjust the tension settings on my sewing machine when I quilt, based on the thickness of the quilt layers. I seldom have to make these adjustments, however, since I usually use either thin or medium-thick battings, which are easy to stitch through.

quilting guide

fig. 7

WALKING FOOT

Changing your standard presser foot to a walking foot is the key to machine-quilting beautifully. A walking foot is used for straight line stitching, as in all the quilting I've done for the projects in this book. It helps to move all three layers forward at the same time. It is especially helpful when you are quilting something a bit bulky, like a paper-pieced top. With a standard presser foot, it's easy to slip on the bulky part, which could result in a distorted top layer. A walking foot does a better job keeping the shape of the quilt top.

MASKING TAPE AND QUILTING GUIDE

To ensure that your stitching is straight, attach a piece of masking tape right next to where you need to stitch. You then sew right along the edge of the tape. Masking tape can be removed easily and can be reused multiple times. The thicker the tape is, the better you can control making a straight guide.

I use a quilting guide to keep the distance between lines of straight quilting stitches uniform (fig.7). Just place it on your sewing machine with your desired width between stitching. Align the quilting guide with the previous row of stitching as you sew. An example of a project where these two tools helped me save time is the You've-Got-Mail Wall Pocket (page 90). When I quilted the main organizer, I started off with a long piece of masking tape that reached from one edge to the other. After stitching right next to the edge of the tape, I removed the tape. Then I set up the quilting guide to do more stitching with the same width throughout. Once I was done with

parallel stitching, I used an acrylic ruler to determine a line that was perpendicular to one of the lines I quilted. I then put the masking tape along the ruler to repeat the same process.

THREADS

I've learned that some threads are much easier to use for quilting than others. After several "quilty" friends of mine gushed over Aurifil 40 wt cotton threads, I started using them to machine-quilt. Yes, they are right about this thread being the best quilting thread. It's very silky and smooth and penetrates three layers of fabric and batting so nicely.

LONGER STITCH LENGTH

As I mentioned earlier, I like my stitch length to be between 2.8 mm to 3.5 mm when I quilt. The stitch length can be long because it simply needs to quilt together three layers so that the batting won't shift. When we make something like a handbag, we want the stitching length to be much shorter so the two layers are tightly stitched together; thus, your bag bottom will not easily tear apart when you place something heavy inside. Because a quilt doesn't get stressed in the same way, we don't have to use short stitches to ensure that it won't fall apart.

QUILTING GLOVES

These are gloves with nonslip material on the palms, which help you have a firmer grip on the fabric layers as you machine-stitch your quilt. I use gardening gloves from a dollar store—they work like a charm!

paper-piecing patchwork technique

In this book, there are several projects that use a paper-piecing method. Paper-piecing is a technique of foundation piecing that uses a piece of paper as a guideline to sew fabric on in a particular order. If you are a beginner and have never tried this method, you may be a little scared of it. But don't worry, it's really not as difficult or complicated as you might think. In fact, you might get hooked on this technique once you know how easily you can achieve a perfectly pieced patchwork. I love this method for the following reasons:

1 IT'S EASY TO ACHIEVE A PERFECT-LOOKING RESULT.
With this technique, your finished result will look flat and clean, just like the drawing on the paper. However detailed your design is, you are absolutely in control of the finished size, as long as you can keep in mind a few simple things that I will explain later. When you are piecing many small pieces of fabric together in a standard way, your finished patchwork is likely to be a little off the size it's supposed to be. This may be caused by the nature of the fabric or by fabric pieces being slightly larger or smaller or your seam allowances being larger or smaller than they are supposed to be. Paper-piecing does not require taking these factors into consideration for a perfect result. You can be lazy and floppy and still achieve a perfect result easily.

2 I CAN SAVE TIME ON CUTTING FABRICS. As I just mentioned, fabric pieces do not need to be cut to an exact size when you are paper-piecing. The only thing to remember is that your fabric piece is a lot larger than the finished size of the piece, as I will discuss later in this section.

3 I DON'T HAVE TO WORRY ABOUT SEAM ALLOWANCES BEING EXACT THROUGHOUT. This technique calls for an adjustment of seam allowances as you go, so you don't need to worry about seam allowances being exactly ¼" (6 mm) throughout.

MUST-HAVE MATERIALS

These are the materials you need to get started.

1 FOUNDATION PAPER. A few types of paper are available, but I use two kinds exclusively: standard copy paper and JT-426 Perfect Piecing by June Tailor. For a project on which I want to remove the paper after the patchwork is complete, I use standard copy paper. This is the most economical option and is readily available. Some examples of projects in this book where I used copy paper are the Swedish Bloom-Time Lap Quilt and the Vintage Pencil Case (pages 82 and 114).

For a project on which I want to leave the paper to stabilize patchwork, I use the Perfect Piecing Quilt Block Foundation Sheets, which I refer to as "paper for foundation" in project instructions. I love this product because it comes in the same size as standard copy paper—8½" × 11" (21.5 × 28 cm). And

just as with standard copy paper, you can print on this paper. It is transparent, so it's easy to see through. Unlike similar products I have tried, this one is quite strong and it is not easily torn with small stitching or distorted by pressing. The My Scrappy Box and the You've-Got-Mail Wall Pocket (pages 76 and 90) are examples of projects in this book where I use this paper and leave it on the back of the patchwork as a stabilizer. You can print on this paper using your printer, or trace patterns with a mechanical pencil.

Every template for paper-piecing in this book is smaller than 8½" × 11" (21.5 × 28 cm), so you will be able to print out all templates using your home printer.

2 ROTARY CUTTER, ACRYLIC RULER, SCISSORS. Before you begin paper-piecing, you will cut your fabric pieces at a size that is at least ¼" (6 mm) larger than the finished size of the piece all around the edges. (I like to make mine at least ¾" (2 cm) larger at all edges just to be safe.) You will need standard scissors for that. A rotary cutter is needed to trim seam allowances as you go. Each time you sew fabric onto paper, you will use an acrylic ruler to measure ¼" (6 mm) from a seam and a rotary cutter to cut off excess.

GREAT-TO-HAVE MATERIALS

3 TEMPORARY ADHESIVE STICK FOR FABRIC. This makes your life so much better! It is not necessary, but it is only a few bucks and is readily available at most craft stores, so I highly

recommend you get one. I use this adhesive to attach fabric onto paper temporarily. For example, I always use it to attach my first fabric piece on a template numbered "1." If you look at the You've-Got-Mail Wall Pocket template (page 90), you will see that piece #1 is the large middle part of the envelope. This adhesive stick will help you control the exact position of the fabric. Place the first piece on the printed template and choose the position you like. Dab this stick on the paper a few times and attach the wrong side of the fabric: when your other fabric pieces are sewn onto it, it will not shift. I also use this stick when it is not easy to press fabric sewn on the paper in the direction it should go. For instance, in the You've-Got-Mail Wall Pocket, when you sew the #9 piece, the #4, #6, and #7 pieces must be folded and pressed flat. Dabbing this adhesive onto the corner on the wrong side of these pieces will keep them flat. Quilting-weight cotton is usually easily pressed and folded, but linen or other thicker fabric often requires some extra effort. Also, when fabric pieces are large, as in the border around the wall pocket, pinning is sufficient. But when pieces are small, it is simply much easier to dab the pieces with this stick a few times to temporarily make the fold nice and flat.

In addition, because this glue is temporary, it has weak adhesiveness. You can reposition fabric several times without making any mess. (You may need to dab on some more glue if you reposition the fabric several times.) If you are not satisfied with where you have placed your fabric piece, simply remove it, dab more adhesive, and reposition

↓ freezer paper

the piece until you are happy with its placement. This "temporary" feature is great, because if you are using copy paper for your paper-pieced projects, you will want to remove the paper, which can be done easily.

4 FREEZER PAPER. There are some paper-pieced projects in this book for which freezer paper can be a great help. It is sold at craft stores and grocery stores. It comes in a big roll, so it will last for a long time! I use freezer paper when I want to control exactly what part of the fabric's print pattern shows in the finished work. For example, if you look at the strawberries book block in the Books-for-Baby Quilt on page 73 (fourth row, fourth column), you see that all elephants are laid out horizontally. (Okay. I admit it isn't perfectly horizontal, but it is sort of, right?) In order to achieve the look, I created a freezer paper template only for that piece . It was important to me to make the elephant part look like one unified background, so I used the freezer paper to make sure all the elephants are matched horizontally to the top edge of the template. Other parts of the elephant background pieces can be easily done without freezer paper because when you sew the pieces, the edge is either horizontal or vertical to the block's edges.

I used the same freezer paper template for other book blocks, like the fish and the grocery ones. If you are using fabric for which placement of a fabric's design doesn't matter—as in solids or small polka dots—a freezer paper template is not necessary. For example, for the pink book block with dotted leaves design, I didn't use my freezer paper template for the #2 in the pink template because the background is simple polka dots (page 73). For fabrics where placement does matter because design has a set flow (horizontally laid out, etc), it's a different story. When using this kind of fabric for any paper-pieced projects where design placement matters, a freezer paper template is a great help.

Another example of a paper-pieced project that requires a freezer paper template is the Triangle Patchwork Box Pouch (page 108). Once again, if you are using solids or all-over prints such as polka dots, you can skip the freezer paper template. However, if you want to control how the design displays in the finished work (especially for fussier designs), a freezer paper template is very useful. For example, the lady on the orange pouch stands nicely straight because I used a freezer paper template to cut the fabric before I sewed it.

paper-piecing

Now let me show you how you can paper-piece a book block for the Books-for-Baby Quilt (page 68). Before you begin, remember the following four points:

1 TEMPLATES ARE ALWAYS MIRROR IMAGES. You will be placing fabric on the WRONG side of the paper (the side without a print pattern). The finished look will be a mirror image of the design on the paper. To make a book facing right, you will need a template with a book design facing left. Most templates I provide in this book don't need to be reversed to make a mirror image. For example, all templates for the Swedish Bloom-Time Lap Quilt (page 82) as well as the You've-Got-Mail Wall Pocket (page 90) are examples of templates that are symmetrical.

2 WRITE THE COLORS/DESIGN ON EACH PIECE OF THE TEMPLATE. I am very used to the paper-piecing technique, but I still often make the mistake of placing fabrics in the wrong order. The more complicated a design is, the more helpful it is to label template pieces to avoid confusion and avoid having to use your seam ripper!

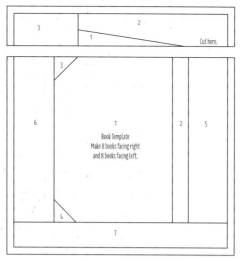
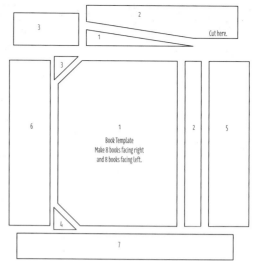

fig. 1

fig. 2

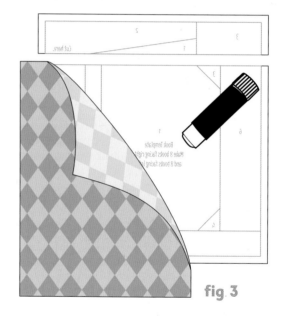

fig. 3

3 IT IS VERY HELPFUL TO PRINT AN EXTRA COPY OF A TEMPLATE (just one for one type of design) and cut these into pieces along the lines. You can use these paper pieces only to ensure that your fabric piece is larger than the piece (finished size). Your fabric piece should be at least ¼" (6mm) larger on all sides than the paper piece.

4 USE A SMALL STITCHING LENGTH, especially if you are using a copy paper that is to be removed. Smaller stitching will allow the fabrics to remain securely sewn when the paper is removed. I like to use very small stitching for short seams (1.0 mm–1.5 mm/stitch for any seam shorter than 2" [5 cm]) and just a little smaller than a standard stitching length for other seams (1.8 mm/stitch).

Now, let's move on to actually piecing the book block:

1 Start by printing the templates on copy paper. One (left side) is to use as a piecing pattern or foundation for sewing. The other (right side) is to cut into pieces. This book block template calls for two sections. Take the one that you will use as a foundation paper and cut right along the line where indicated (**fig. 1**). You can start with either section, but in this tutorial, I started with the bottom piece.

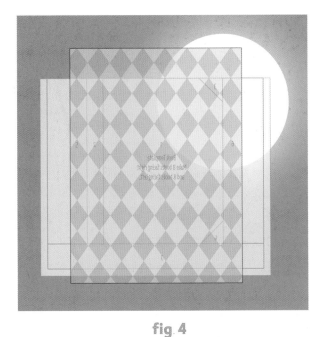

fig. 4

fig. 5

Sew on the line
between 1 and 2.

Book Template
Make 8 books facing right
and 8 books facing left.

fig. 6

fig. 7

2 As you can see, the cut paper piece is a pattern to ensure the size of your fabric piece. In this image, I have a paper piece numbered #1. I placed it on the fabric that I want to use for #1, with the right sides together. Notice that the fabric piece is at least ¼" (6 mm) larger than the paper piece along the edges (fig. 2)!

3 Use glue to temporarily attach this fabric piece. Note that the glue is applied on the WRONG side

of the paper and that the WRONG side of the fabric is attached to it (fig. 3).

4 If you have a light box, place the paper piece numbered #2 on its surface. Then place the fabric piece over the paper to check that there is at least ¼" (6 mm) of additional margin for a seam allowance (fig. 4). I use sunlight during the daytime and a ceiling light at night as my "light box."

5 With the right sides together, fold the paper (only the paper) along the line between #1 and #2 pieces. Use a ruler and a rotary cutter to add a neat ¼" (6 mm) seam allowance on the fabric for fabric piece #1 (fig. 5).

6 Now place a fabric for #2. Note that there is only one edge that is rotary cut—the edge that is aligned with fabric piece #1 (fig. 6).

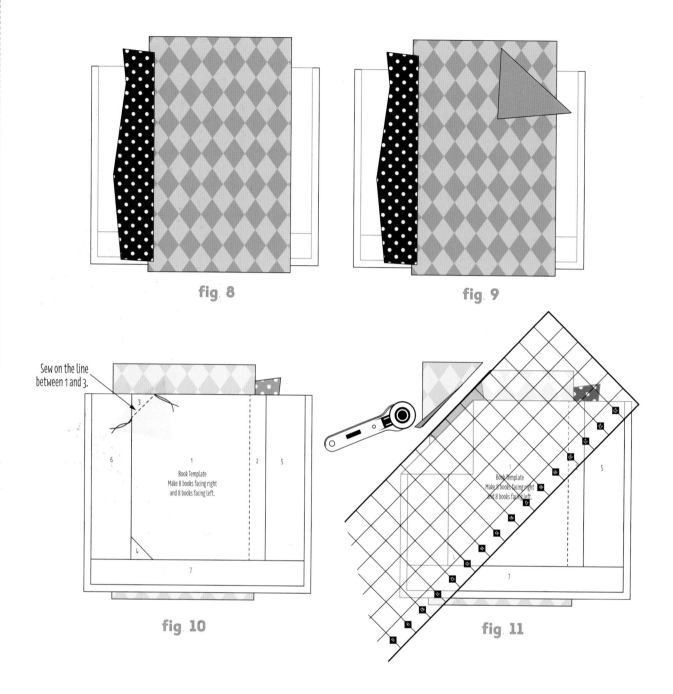

fig. 8

fig. 9

Sew on the line between 1 and 3.

Book Template
Make 8 books facing right
and 8 books facing left.

fig. 10

Book Template
Make 8 books facing right
and 8 books facing left.

fig. 11

7 Pin in place and turn the paper. Sew on the line between #1 and #2 (fig. 7).

8 Turn the paper and press with an iron to make the #2 fabric cover the area on the #2 paper piece (fig. 8).

9 You can use a ruler and a rotary cutter to cut the #1 fabric in the way I did in Step 5. But if you are a little lazy like me, you can skip the cutting process here, because the #3 triangle is so small that you know it is very likely that you have a large enough fabric piece for it (fig. 9).

10+11 Sew along the line between #1 and #3 (fig. 10). Fold the paper and trim the excess fabric (fig. 11).

12 In the same manner as in Steps 10 and 11, sew another brown corner #4 (fig. 12).

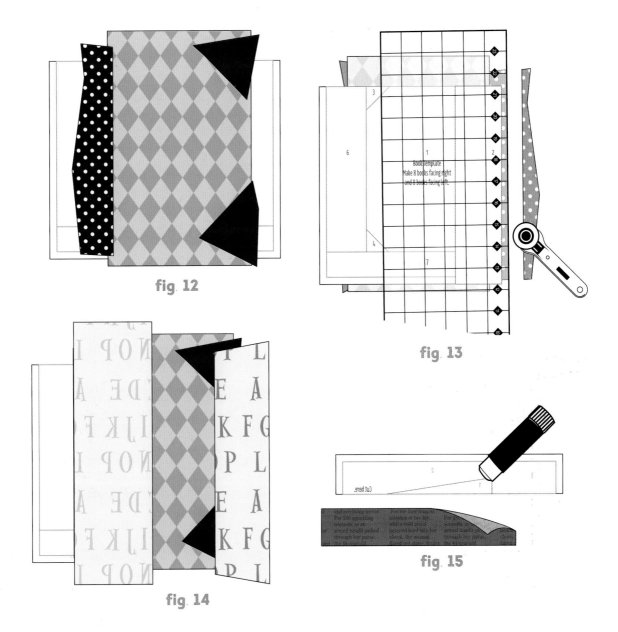

fig. 12

fig. 13

fig. 14

fig. 15

13 Before sewing piece #5, make sure that this edge is straight (fig. 13).

14 Place the fabric piece for area #5, making sure that the edges are nicely aligned to ensure that the background fabric with its alphabet print will align neatly with the block edges (fig. 14).

15 Sew, press with an iron, and trim the excess fabric.

16 Once the last piece is sewn, trim excess fabric at all edges. It is important to remember to leave a ¼" (6 mm) seam allowance along all edges.

17 To start the second section of the block, once again start with glue (fig. 15).

18 This time, don't fold the paper to cut off the excess fabric. (You can if you choose, but it's a bit challenging to fold along the line and I prefer to adjust the seam allowance later.)

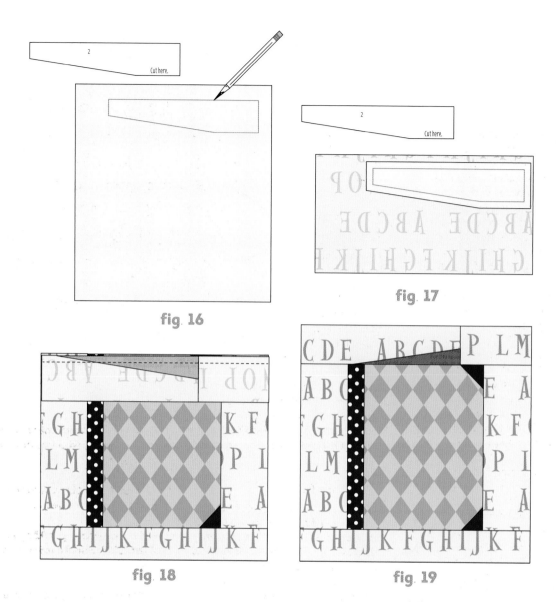

fig. 16

fig. 17

fig. 18

fig. 19

19+20 Make a freezer paper template for this piece. The freezer paper template includes ¼" (6 mm) seam allowances along all edges (fig. 16).

21 Make this template by tracing the #2 paper piece with the right side up, thus creating a mirror image (fig. 17). Gently press this piece onto the wrong side of the fabric. (If you are using the same freezer paper template for book blocks facing the other side, you will press this paper on the right side of the fabric.) Trim excess fabric.

22 Now, sew the fabric piece onto the paper foundation; press. Trim the excess.

23 Sew the last fabric piece onto the paper. Cut off the excess fabric. Now you have two sections complete.

24 Gently remove the paper.

25 Sew the two sections together and press open the seam (fig. 18).

26 Your book block is complete (fig. 19)!

binding

Quite a few of the projects in this book include binding raw edges. By binding the raw edge of a piece of fabric, we can ensure that the edge does not fray with use. A binding tape in a contrasting color adds a nice design touch to the project. I made all the binding tapes that I used for the projects in this book. You can purchase pre-made binding tapes at local craft and fabric stores, but I highly recommend you make your own binding tapes. You'll have much wider fabric options from which to choose!

A binding tape can be made by sewing long strips of fabric together. The width of the strip is based on the desired width of the finished tape, as well as the thickness of the project. The width and length of the strips to cut are included in the instructions for each project. Fabric strips can be cut either on the bias of the fabric or parallel or perpendicular to the selvedge of the fabric. When you are making a binding tape to finish a curvy edge (for example, in the Yum-Yum Apple Bib, page 60), the binding should be made from fabric cut on the bias, since fabric strips cut on the bias are stretchy and bind curved edges beautifully. Many quilters prefer to make all binding tape strips from fabrics cut on the bias (fig. 1). But you can also cut strips parallel or perpendicular to the selvedge, which is easier and more economical since it wastes little or no fabric. Whenever you make a binding tape for your project, remember to make it quite a bit longer than necessary. Should you discover that your binding tape is too short after you finish sewing it to your project edges, you'll see that it is more work to sew additional strips to lengthen the binding tape than if you had started with an extra-long piece of tape to avoid piecing it. However, if the tape is longer than needed, you can cut off the excess and toss it into your scrap box!

SINGLE FOLD

A single-fold binding tape is made from a strip that is four times wider than a finished tape on one side of the project. [1" (2.5 cm) width strip to make ¼" (6 mm) wide tape on one side.] Tools for making binding tape save a lot of time and form evenly folded edges. They are available at craft and fabric stores.

DOUBLE FOLD

A double-fold binding tape creates two layers of fabric folded over the edge of your project. These binding strips are much wider; however, this binding tape is thick and strong. I find double-fold binding tape easier to attach for a nice finish.

raw-edged appliqué

A few projects in this book include appliqués with raw edges, meaning that the edge is not folded under like those of a needle-turn appliqué. I like raw-edged appliqué because it is easy and quick. Here is a process for creating raw-edged appliqués whose edges won't unravel.

fig. 1

{ a little advice }
If you are a visual learner like me and prefer to learn techniques visually rather than just from reading, I highly recommend you search for online video tutorials. Search by name of the technique you want to learn on YouTube, for instance. You will probably find at least a few free videos where someone does a great job of explaining the technique while demonstrating it.

1 Place a fusible webbing piece on top of a pattern with its paper-ish side on top.

2 Trace the pattern onto the webbing with a pencil.

3 Cut the webbing, adding at least ⅛" (3 mm) allowance on all edges.

4 Place the sticky side of the webbing on the wrong side of the fabric and iron to fuse, following the manufacturer's instructions.

5 After the fusible webbing cools, cut right along the traced line with scissors.

6 Remove the paper backing.

7 Position the appliqué on the background fabric with the wrong sides together and fuse.

for the Kitchen

materials (for 1 coaster)

Cotton print on white background
○ One 5½" × 6" (14 × 15 cm) rectangle
  for bell center

Cotton print with typography
○ One 5½" × 4" (14 × 10 cm) rectangle

Cotton geometric print
One 5½" × 4" (14 × 10 cm) rectangle
○ One 6" × 8" (15 × 20.5 cm) rectangle
  for backing

Brown felt
○ One ½" × 2½" (1.3 × 6.5 cm) rectangle
  for stem

Cotton batting
○ One 5¾" × 7¾" (14.5 × 19.5 cm) rectangle

tools

Basic Quilting Tools (page 11)
Fabric marker

Bell Pepper Coaster

This coaster is a quick, fun, and unique project! Select three fabric scraps in the same colorway and, in a short period of time, turn them into a coaster shaped like a fancy bell pepper! Although you are sewing curvy lines, you will not be piecing curvy seams—that can be a hard and time-consuming process. This project is designed so that you won't even have to deal with handstitching. It is great for newbies who are not comfortable with advanced techniques but don't want to make something too simple. Like me, you'll want to make several!

difficulty: ★

finished size: 4½" (longest part) × 4⅝" (widest part)
(11.5 × 11.7 cm) without stem

create a coaster

1 With the right sides together, fold the cotton print on white background in half lengthwise. Trace the center template for the bell pepper [fig. 1] in the middle on one wrong side of the fabric.

2 Sew the folded fabric along the traced line using small stitches (1.5 mm–1.8 mm), stitching the curved parts slowly and carefully. Sew around all edges.

3 Trim excess fabric, leaving a ⅛" (3 mm) seam allowance around all edges; clip the seam at the curves, making sure not to cut through stitching.

Templates are actual size

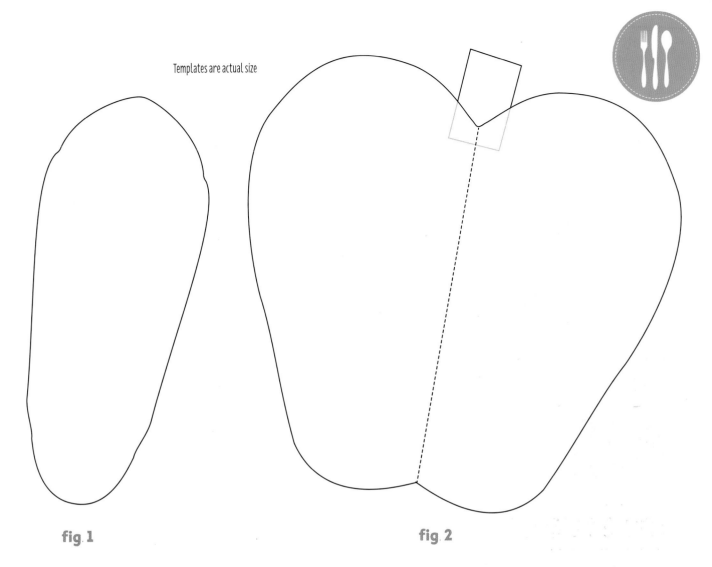

fig. 1

fig. 2

4 Slit one side of the fabric in the center to make a 1½" (3.8 cm) long opening. Turn the piece right side out through the opening. Iron to press and set it aside.

5 For the front side pieces: with the right sides together, stitch the two cotton print rectangles (geometric and typographic) using a ¼" (6 mm) seam allowance. Press the seam open. On the wrong side of this piece, trace the bell pepper (fig. 2), making sure that the dotted line of the template is centered over the sewn seam.

6 Place the piece in Step 5 on top of the cotton print for backing with right sides together.

Underneath the cotton print for backing, add cotton batting to create three layers. Pin in place and sew along the traced line to stitch the three layers together in the shape of the bell pepper. Again, use small stitches to sew curved lines more easily. Trim excess fabric to leave a ⅛" (3 mm) seam allowance all around. Clip the curves in several places.

7 With a seam ripper, create a 1½" (3.8 cm) long opening in the seam of the front piece. Turn the piece right side out through the opening. Press.

8 Using matching thread, topstitch around all edges for a finished look.

9 Fold the felt piece in half widthwise and place on the top part of the front piece, overlapping by ¼" (6 mm) (refer to fig. 2). Handbaste to the front piece, close to the short edges of the felt.

10 Place the bell pepper center piece right side up in the middle of the front piece, aligning seam openings. Pin in place and topstitch around the center piece to attach. For the top thread, use a color that matches the bell pepper center fabric; for the bobbin thread, use a color that matches the backing fabric.

materials (for 3 towels)

Linen
- Three 19½" × 26" (49.5 × 66 cm) rectangles for towel base

Cotton prints, assorted
- Thirteen scraps for Breakfast towel
- Ten scraps for Lunch towel
- Eight scraps for Dinner towel
- Three fat quarters for binding tapes [or seven 2" × 18" (5 × 45.5 cm) strips]

Three 5" (12.5 cm) long rickrack tapes

Cotton thread to match assorted cotton prints

Two 12" × 9" (30.5 × 23 cm) sheets of fusible web

tools

Basic Quilting Tools (page 11)

note

All seam allowances are ½" (1.3 cm), unless otherwise indicated.

Breakfast, Lunch & Dinner Towels

I love the look of cotton print appliqués on linen because the textured feel of linen helps the smooth appliqué fabric stand out nicely. Select cotton print scraps that contrast with the color of your linen, then enjoy creating letters to form fun words on your towels! My favorite cotton prints to use for this project are feedsack fabric and small-scale allover prints.

difficulty: ★ ★
finished size: 19½" × 26" (49.5 × 66 cm)

appliqué the fabric scraps

1 Trace the letters {fig. 1} onto the paper backing of the fusible web. Cut the three words apart and work with one word at a time. Roughly cut out the individual letters in one word, leaving a small margin of fusible web around the edges. (See Raw-Edged Appliqué, page 27.)

2 Following the manufacturer's instructions, fuse a letter to the wrong side of each fabric scrap. Cut out the letters, following the tracings. Remove the paper backing from each letter.

3 Position the letters on the main linen rectangle, arranging them as shown on page 34 and above right, or as desired. Fuse the letters to the linen.

4 Using thread that matches or coordinates with each letter, machine-appliqué the letters to the linen. Use a zigzag stitch 1.0 mm wide and 2.5 mm long.

5 Repeat the same process with kitchen patterns. For the Breakfast towel, appliqué a frying pan, a sunny-side-up egg, and a spatula {fig. 2}. For the Lunch towel, appliqué salt and pepper shakers {fig. 3, page 38}. For the Dinner towel, appliqué a pot and a ladle {fig. 4, page 39}.

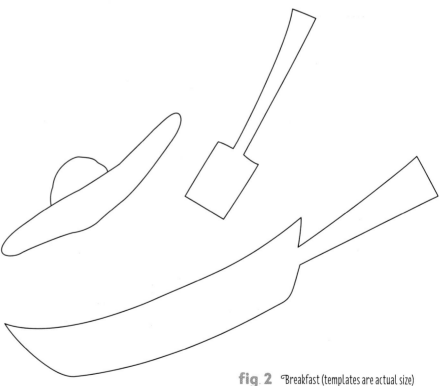

fig. 2 Breakfast (templates are actual size)

DINNER

BREAKFAST

LUNCH

fig. 1 (print at 167%)

finish towels

6 Make a loop to hang the towel. Baste a rickrack piece approximately 3½" (9 cm) from the top left corner on the wrong side of the linen body (see photo above for placement).

7 Create a bias binding tape. To make a bias tape, cut out an 18" × 18" (45.5 × 45.5 cm) square from a cotton print fat quarter. Fold the piece to make a diagonal crease from one corner to another. Unfold and cut along the folded line. Right sides together, place one of the triangles on top of the other, aligning straight-grain edges. Stitch along the edge. Press seam open. Draw lines parallel to short edges, leaving 2" (5 cm) spacing between each. Make a loop by matching long edges. Make sure that the first line at one edge is matched with the second line at the other edge. Sew along the edge. Press seam open

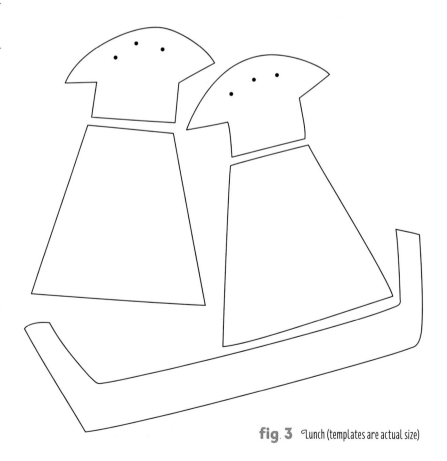

fig. 3 Lunch (templates are actual size)

and cut along the drawn lines. This will bind one linen towel.

8 Fold the tape you just created in half lengthwise, wrong sides together. Press. Open and fold two long edges toward the folded line. Press. Make sure that one long edge is aligned with the folded line, but the other long edge is about ⅛"–¼" (3–6 mm) away from the folded edge. This will ensure that you will catch the bias tape when you topstitch the binding with the front on top. Press again and unfold.

9 Place one long edge of the bias strip on top of the linen [the one that is ½" (1.3 cm) from the folded line] next to the middle of a side edge. Leave 2" (5 cm) margin from the short edge and start machine-sewing along the folded line so you are sewing a line that is ½" (1.3 cm) away from the edge of the linen. When you are about 2" (5 cm) from the short edge of the binding tape, backstitch and stop sewing the binding tape to the linen. Use a ruler to determine the length needed for a seam on the short ends, and cut off the excess. Sew the short ends together and finish sewing it to the

linen. See Binding on page 26 for more details.

10 Miter and handbaste all four corners on the wrong side of the linen towel.

11 Topstitch on the binding tape, making sure that you are catching the binding tape on the back as well.

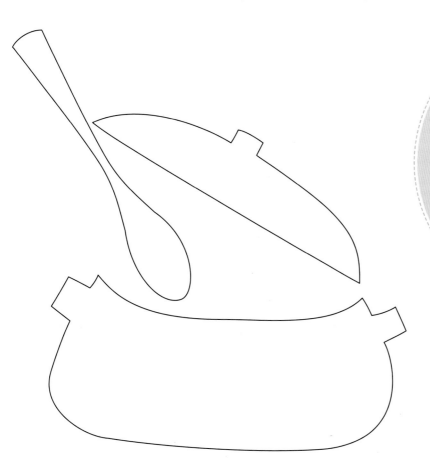

{ note } You can create a straight-grain tape instead of a bias tape. Just use strips cut on the straight grain. Place the short edge of one strip's right side on top of the short end of another. Stitch along the seam. Repeat the process to make a continuous binding tape.

fig. 4 Dinner (templates are actual size)

materials

Cotton solid
- One 7" × 14" (18 × 35.5 cm) rectangle for front exterior
- One 10" × 14" (25.5 × 35.5 cm) rectangle for back exterior

Cotton print
- Two 12" × 14" (30.5 × 35.5 cm) rectangles for lining

Assorted cotton print and solid scraps
- Many scraps, ranging from 1" × 1" (2.5 × 2.5 cm) to 3" × 3" (7.5 × 7.5 cm)

Cotton print
- Two 12½" × 2½" (31.5 × 6.5) strips for binding tape

Cotton print
- One 3" × 2½" (7.5 × 6.5 cm) rectangle for top loop

Insulated batting
- Two 12" × 14" (30.5 × 35.5 cm) rectangles

Crocheted cherries by Riley Blake Designs *(optional)*

Crocheted lace trim *(optional)*
- One 25" (63.5 cm) piece [⅜" (1 cm) wide shown]

tools

Basic Quilting Tools (page 11)
Quilting adhesive spray

note

All seam allowances are ¼" (6 cm), unless otherwise indicated.

Lettered Tea Cozy

There is something so fun and rewarding about paper-piecing alphabets! This tea cozy features the paper-pieced word "TEA" and a teacup. Luckily, all the letters in TEA are very simple to piece! Use striking colors for the letters, a print for the teacup, and a contrasting solid for the background fabric. Insulated batting will help keep your teapot nice and warm. If you are making this as a gift for a tea-loving friend, how about adding a little teabag pouch (page 46) with her favorite tea in it?

difficulty: ★ ★ ★
finished size: 12" × 10" (30.5 × 25.5 cm)

assemble tea cozy

1 Refer to the paper-piecing method on page 19 to complete four blocks: T, E, A, and a teacup (fig. 1). Each block should measure approximately 3½" × 3¼" (9 × 8.5 cm) unfinished.

2 Sew these blocks together to create a patchwork panel (use the photo on page 40 for reference). The panel should measure approximately 12½" × 3¼" (31.5 × 8.5 cm). Set it aside.

3 Apply adhesive spray thoroughly on the wrong sides of the front and back exterior pieces, and adhere them to the batting. Make sure that one long edge of the rectangle pieces is aligned with one long edge of the batting. There will be 5" (12.5 cm) of exposed batting below the piece.

4 Attach the lining to the other side of the batting in the same manner. There should now be no exposed batting on that side.

5 With the front exterior piece on top, quilt a grid of equally spaced diagonal lines. [Mine are ¾" (6 mm) apart.] See the photo on page 40 for reference.

6 With right sides together, place the pieced panel from Step 2 on top of the quilted layer. Align the top edge of the panel with the bottom edge of the quilted layer and sew along the edge through batting and lining.

7 Turn the panel down so it is right side up on top of the batting, below the quilted cotton solid.

Press and quilt the pieced panel as desired.

8 Assemble the remaining lining, back exterior piece, and batting. Align the back exterior piece so that 2" (5 cm) of batting remains exposed on the bottom. Quilt in the same manner as in Step 5.

9 Using the half template on page 45 (fig. 2), trace a full template onto a large piece of paper such as wrapping paper or freezer paper. Cut out and place the full template on top of the front panel, making sure you have an extra ¾" (2 cm) of exposed batting at the bottom edge. Trace and cut along the pattern line. Repeat for the back panel.

10 Fold the fabric piece for the top loop in half widthwise, creasing in the middle. Fold two outer edges toward the center crease, wrong sides together, and press. Fold the piece in half again so that you have a folded piece

{ tip }
This instructions call for an exposed seam allowance inside the tea cozy. If you would like to cover up the seam allowance, you can bind it after Step 11.

measuring ¾" × 2½" (2 × 6.5 cm). Topstitch along both long edges. Fold in half widthwise. Using a small seam allowance, machine-baste this piece at the top of the right side of the front panel. The short edges of the loop piece will be aligned with the top seam of the front panel.

11 With the right sides together, sew the front and back panels together along the curved edge. Turn right side out. Set aside.

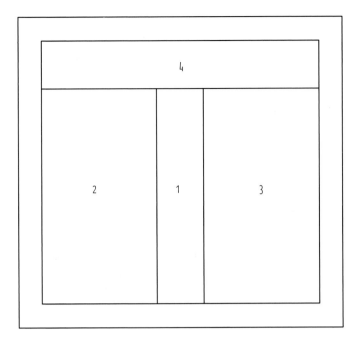

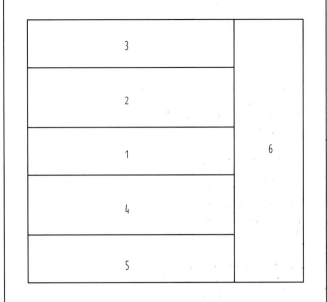

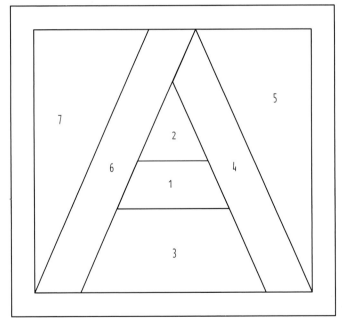

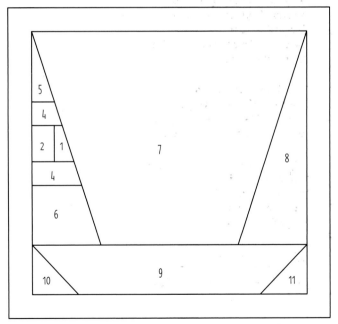

fig. 1

Templates are actual size

12 With the right sides together, place one binding tape strip on top of the other. Sew both short edges together to create a loop. With the wrong sides together, fold and press ¼" (6 mm) from one long edge all the way around the binding loop.

13 Pin the binding around the tea cozy with the right sides together, matching the raw (unfolded) edge of the binding to the bottom edge of the exterior fabric. Make sure to match the seams of the binding loop with the seams of the exterior fabric. Turn the tea cozy wrong side out. Sew the unfolded edge of the binding to the tea cozy.

14 Wrap the folded edge of the binding over the edge of the tea cozy and handstitch to the lining. The binding should be approximately 1" (2.5 cm) wide.

15 Handstitch the crocheted cherries close to the top of the tea cozy as desired.

16 Handstitch (or fuse) lace to the exterior of the cozy, aligning with top edge of binding.

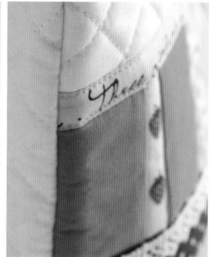

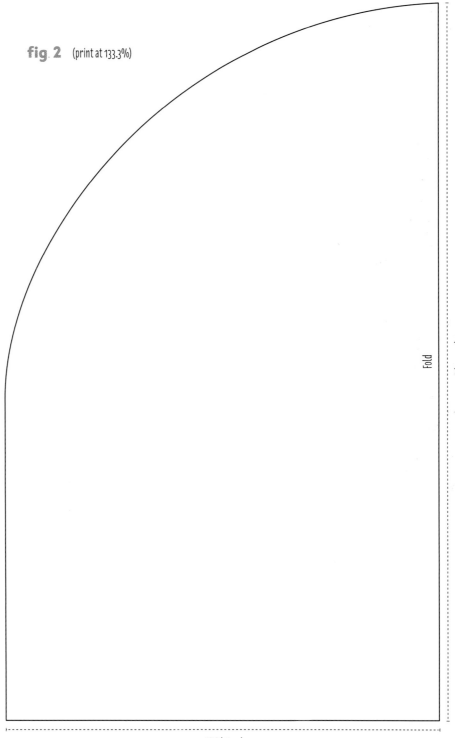

fig. 2 (print at 133.3%)

Fold

10" (25.5 cm)

6¼" (16 cm)

materials

Cotton print
- One 3¾" × 11.5" (9.5 × 29 cm) rectangle for exterior

Cotton solid
- One 3¾" × 11.5" (9.5 × 29 cm) rectangle for interior

Assorted cotton solids
- Three 3¾" × 2¼" (9.5 × 5.5 cm) rectangles for pockets

Assorted cotton prints
- Three 3¾" × 3¼" (9.5 × 8.5 cm) rectangles for pockets

Lightweight fusible interfacing
- Three 3⅛" × 2⅛" (8 × 5.25 cm) rectangles for pockets
- One 3⅛" × 10⅞" (8 × 27.75 cm) rectangle for exterior

One small button

2" (5 cm) long string

Teabag Pouch

finished size: 3¼" W × 11" H (8.5 × 28 cm)

1 With the right sides together, stitch along the top edges of one solid pocket piece and one print pocket piece. Match the bottom long

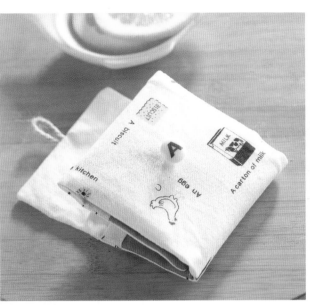

edge of the pieces and sew together. From the side openings, turn the piece right side out.

2 Press the bottom of the piece so that the piece is folded at the bottom seam. The print piece is 1" (2.5 cm) longer than the solid, so place it on top before you sew the edge; stitch. The print will be ½" (1.3 cm) high at the top of the front pocket; press.

3 Through side opening, insert lightweight interfacing pocket piece. The sticky side should be facing the solid part (front). Make sure it is approximately in the middle. Fuse. Repeat Steps 1–3 to make the middle pocket.

4 For the last pocket, sew only the top edge of the solid piece to the print piece. Align the bottom edge of the solid with the bottom edge of the cotton print, right sides together. Press the whole piece; you will see that this piece has ½" (1.3 cm) high print on the front as well. Unfold the piece, place the interfacing right below the fold in the middle, and iron to fuse.

Fold it in half with the wrong sides together again.

5 At the bottom edge of the rectangle, align the bottom edge of the pocket from Step 4, front side up. Pin in place and machine-baste three edges (except for the top edge) of the pocket using a scant ⅛" (3 mm) seam allowance.

6 Position the middle pocket piece where its bottom edge and the top edge of the bottom pocket are approximately 1" (2.5 cm) apart. Pin in place and machine-baste both short edges. Then edgestitch the bottom edge of the pocket.

7 Repeat with the remaining pocket so that three pockets are attached to the interior rectangle with 1" (2.5 mm) space between each pocket.

8 Fuse the interfacing onto the back of the exterior fabric, approximately in the middle. At the top edge, machine-baste the string. The edges of the string should be aligned to the middle of the top seam.

9 With the right sides together, sew the exterior and interior together, leaving about a 2" (5 cm) wide opening along one side. Trim all four corners. Turn right side out through the opening. Use a point-turner, chopstick, or other instrument to push out the corners. Press well. Slipstitch the opening closed.

10 Insert teabags into each of the three pockets and fold the piece up, bottom part first. Lightly mark where the string loop naturally lies and handsew the button onto the exterior fabric.

materials

Twill

○ One 24" × 17" (61 × 43 cm) rectangle
[This includes 1" (2.5 cm) seam allowance for width and 2½" (6.5 cm) seam allowance for height. Adjust measurements as desired.]

○ One 6½" × 18½" (16.5 × 47 cm) rectangle for pocket lining

Assorted cotton prints

○ Scraps for patchwork blocks

Cotton print

○ Two 4" × 34" (10 × 86.5 cm) strips for straps *[This includes 1" (2.5 cm) seam allowance total for short edges. Adjust length as desired.]*

Cotton print

○ One 2" × 18½" (5 × 47 cm) strip for pocket binding

Ribbon for embellishment *(optional)*

tools

Basic Quilting Tools (page 11)

note

All seam allowances are ¼" (6 cm), unless otherwise indicated.

The Polka-Dot-Café Apron

This is a playful but practical apron with a patchwork pocket in the middle. Customize the fit of your apron by adjusting the width and length of the straps. Select some favorite prints from your fabric stash and make three patchwork blocks for the pocket.

difficulty: ★ ★

finished size: 23 × 14½" (58.5 × 37 cm), each strap: 33" (84 cm) long

create the patchwork pocket

1 Make one block at a time. Using the pattern templates provided {figs. 1–4}, cut out squares and triangles from print scraps. These can be positioned on the right side of the fabric and ironed for temporary attachment. Cut the fabric along the template edges and remove the template. If you are using fabric with motif designs, this method makes it very easy to position each piece where you want it to be in the finished patchwork block (known as "fussy cutting"). This also saves you time you would otherwise spend on marking lines. Sew in the order shown and press seams {fig. 5, page 53}. The finished block will be a 6½" (16.5 cm) square. Repeat to make two more blocks.

2 Choose the placement of the three blocks and sew them together on the inside vertical edges to form one horizontal patchwork panel. Press seams open.

3 With the right sides facing, sew the patchwork panel to the twill pocket lining rectangle along both short edges and the bottom long edge. Press seams open.

4 Turn panel right side out. Press, pin in place, and edgestitch around the big squares in the patchwork design using a matching thread. Set aside.

5 Create a binding for the pocket. With the wrong sides together, fold the binding strip in half lengthwise. Align this long raw edge, right sides facing, with the

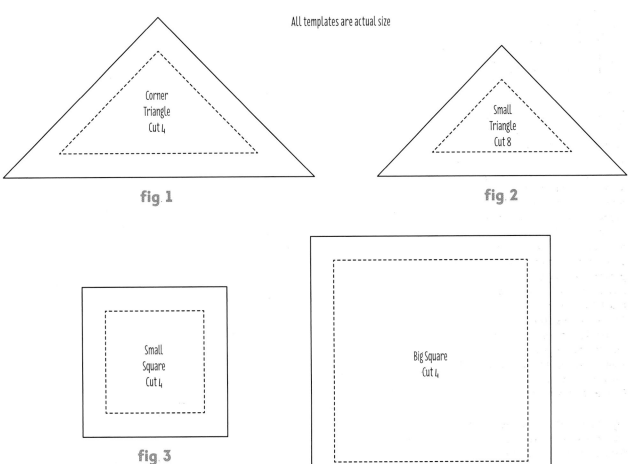

All templates are actual size

Corner
Triangle
Cut 4

fig. 1

Small
Triangle
Cut 8

fig. 2

Small
Square
Cut 4

fig. 3

Big Square
Cut 4

fig. 4

top edge of the patchwork pocket, making sure that the binding is ¼" (6 mm) longer at both short edges. Sew along the long edge. Fold the short edges of the binding inward, bring the folded long edge to the lining of the pocket, and handstitch to finish attaching the binding. Make sure that you are catching only the backing when you handstitch so that it will not be visible on the patchwork panel.

make straps

6 Take one strip for the apron strap and fold ¼" (6 mm) at one short edge with wrong sides together. Fold this strip in half lengthwise, press, and unfold. Fold long edges toward the folded line with the wrong sides together, press, and fold the strip in half

again lengthwise so that the strip measures 1" (2.5 cm) wide.

7 Topstitch all edges except for the raw short edge. Repeat Steps 6 and 7 to complete the second strip.

make apron

8 Fold and press ¼" (6 mm) of the bottom edge of the large twill rectangle for the main apron. Fold the edge again 1" (2.5 cm) from the folded edge.

9 Topstitch close to both the upper and the lower folded edges to finish the bottom edge of the main apron.

10 Fold and press ¼" (6 mm) of one side edge of the main apron with the wrong sides together, then repeat so that you are creating a double fold measuring ¼" (6 mm). Pin in place. Topstitch close to the edge that you folded last. Repeat for the other side.

11 Repeat Step 8 for the top of the main apron. Take one short raw edge of one strap and place it inside the fold, with roughly ½"–¾" (1.3–2 cm) of the edge inside the fold, and pin in place. Repeat for the other strap. Topstitch all edges of the fold on the top edge of the apron.

12 Place the pocket panel in the center 2¾" (7 cm) from the bottom edge of the apron. If desired, insert a folded ribbon under the left short edge of the pocket close to the left bottom corner, tucking its short raw edges under the pocket.

13 Topstitch the short edges and the bottom edge of the pocket onto the apron. Make sure to start about ½" (1.3 cm) away from the top edge at both short edges and backstitch to attach the pocket securely.

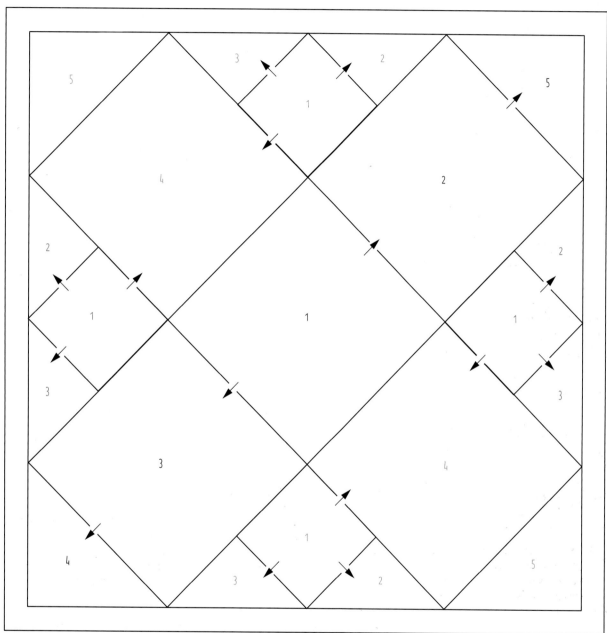

Arrows indicate seam allowance pressing direction.

fig. 5 Template is actual size

materials

Linen
- One 12" × 12" (30.5 × 30.5 cm) square for center piece
- One fat quarter for patchwork

Assorted cotton prints
- Eight square scraps measuring at least 2½" × 2½" (6.5 × 6.5 cm) each

Cotton print
- One 20" × 14" (51 × 35.5 cm) rectangle for backing and binding

Two 12" (30.5 cm) long rickrack trims *(optional)*

tools

Basic Quilting Tools (page 11)

Quilting adhesive spray

8½" × 11" (21.5 × 28 cm) copy paper for paper-piecing *(optional)*

note

All seam allowances are ½" (1.3 cm), unless otherwise indicated.

Diamond Patchwork Placemat

A pretty placemat can make food tastier and mealtimes more enjoyable! This placemat has eight squares for you to showcase your favorite fabrics. The patchwork parts of the placemat are sewn onto backing fabric to protect them from being damaged by laundering—a good thing, since you'll want to make a set and use them all the time.

difficulty: ★ ★ ★

finished size: 18" × 12" (45.5 × 30.5 cm)

assemble patchwork layer

1 Arrange and rearrange the small print squares on the linen fat quarter until you are happy with the layout. Using a paper-piecing method (page 19) or other preferred patchwork method, piece squares to linen triangles to create two patchwork panels, following the template on page 57 (fig. 1). If you are using any directional prints, indicate on the paper squares which corner of the piece should be placed at the top. Include ½" (1.3 cm) seam allowances. Each finished patchwork panel should measure approximately 3¾" × 12" (9.5 × 30.5 cm). Press. Gently remove paper templates.

2 Take a patchwork panel that will be placed on the right of the placemat center piece and trim ¼" (6 mm) from the left long edge to shorten the seam allowance on that edge. Repeat for the other patchwork panel on its right long edge.

3 If desired, add rickrack trim by spraying some adhesive onto the back of the rickrack lengths and attaching each of them at both inside edges of the linen center piece. See photo on page 54 for placement.

4 With the right sides together, sew patchwork panels to the linen center piece with the side edges aligned. Press seam allowance toward patchwork sides. Edgestitch with a ⅛" (3 mm) seam allowance.

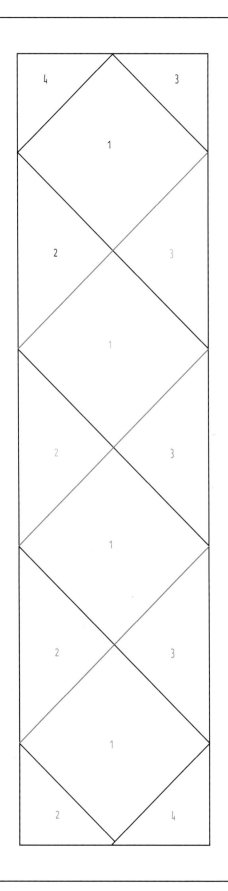

fig. 1
(print at 133.3%)

5 Spray adhesive thoroughly on the wrong side of the placemat top and secure it to the wrong side of the backing fabric. The backing fabric should be 1" (2.5 cm) larger than the placemat top along all edges (trim if necessary).

6 Quilt around all 8 squares. This will keep the patchwork stable.

7 Fold the bottom edge of the backing fabric so that the edge aligns with the bottom edge of the placemat top. Press. Fold the bottom edge to make a ½" (1.3 cm) wide double-fold and press. Pin in place and topstitch very close to the folded edge. The stitching should not exceed ½" (1.3 cm) from both side edges of the placemat top. Repeat the same process with the top edge. Fold all four corners so that the edges of the backing fabric are aligned with the side edges of the placemat top. Press. Make double-folds at both side edges in the same manner that you made double-folds at the top and bottom edges, and handstitch the mitered corners (see lower right photo on page 56).

for kids

materials (for one bib)

Assorted cotton prints
○ Three 3" × 10" (7.5 × 25.5 cm) rectangles for bib front

Contrasting cotton solid
(or store-bought binding tape)
○ One fat quarter for binding tape and straps

Cotton flannel
○ One 8" × 10" (20.5 × 25.5 cm) rectangle for bib back

Assorted green cotton prints/solids
○ Three scraps, each measuring at least 3" × 3" (7.5 × 7.5 cm), for leaf front and back

Brown cotton print
○ One scrap measuring at least 2" × 2" (5 × 5 cm) for seeds

Cotton print matching or contrasting with straps
○ Two 1½" × 1" (3.8 × 2.5 cm) for strap ends

Hook and loop tape (optional)
○ Two 1½" × 1" (3.8 × 2.5 cm) for strap ends

Fusible web for seeds

tools

Basic Quilting Tools (page 11)

Tailor's chalk *(optional)*

note

All seam allowances are ½" (1.3 cm), unless otherwise indicated.

You may prefer to use an easy-opening Velcro closure instead of straps that tie, for convenience and added safety.

Yum-Yum Apple Bib

This adorable bib for babies and toddlers is shaped like a yummy apple. The bib front is made of absorbent cotton, and the backing is a comfy flannel.

difficulty: ★ ★ ★

finished size: 9¼" (widest part) × 7¼" (longest) (23 × 18.5 cm), each strap 12½" (31.5) long

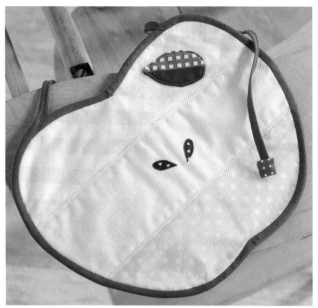

assemble bib

1 Sew three cotton print rectangles together to create one patchwork panel; press open seams. Place this panel onto flannel backing, with the wrong sides together, and sew close to both sides of each patchwork seam, using thread that matches the cotton prints.

2 Fold the panel in half and pin apple template (fig. 1) to the panel, aligning panel sections as shown; cut out. Mark the points with a tailor tack or tailor's chalk, as indicated by the dot on the template.

3 Make a piece of 1" × 6" (2.5 × 15 cm) bias binding tape by cutting on the diagonal of the solid fabric (use a straight ruler and a rotary cutter to make this uniform). This will be a binding tape for the top edge of the bib. Place one short edge of the tape, on the point marked on the left, onto the right side of the apple-shaped

panel. From that point, sew the binding around the apple until the other short edge of the binding tape reaches the other mark. Since you are sewing curvy lines, it's helpful to use many pins. It is easier to work one side at a time: pin only the left half of the bib first, sew to the center point, and backstitch. Next, pin the binding onto the right half of the bib and repeat as on the left. The short edge of the binding should arrive near the point you had marked (if needed, trim the end to make sure that the short edge ends at the mark). Attach the binding tape to the back by handstitching to finish.

4 Make a piece of 1" × 58" (2.5 × 147.5 cm) bias binding tape. Fold this tape in half widthwise to determine the midpoint. Match the midpoint on the binding tape to the center of the bib's bottom edge. Pin this binding to just one half of the bib and sew from the center point to the point where ¼" (6 mm) of the binding tape overlaps the previously attached binding tape on the top. Repeat on the other half of the bib.

Fold the binding tape to the back and handstitch in place.

5 Make straps from the binding tape ends that hang on the top. Fold two long edges to the middle; press, fold lengthwise again, and sew the folds together close to the edge. Start sewing from the raw short edge and finish sewing when you reach the main body of the bib; backstitch. Repeat for the other binding tape.

6 Measure straps and cut them to 12½" (31.5 cm) long each.

7 Fold one of the print pieces for the strap ends in half lengthwise; press. Open and fold two outer edges toward the folded line in the middle lengthwise. Fold ½" (1.3 cm) from each short edge toward the underside, and fold the piece in half widthwise. Press. Sandwich the strap end into the piece so that the end is completely covered by the folded short edge. Handstitch all open edges to complete attaching. Repeat the process for the other strap end.

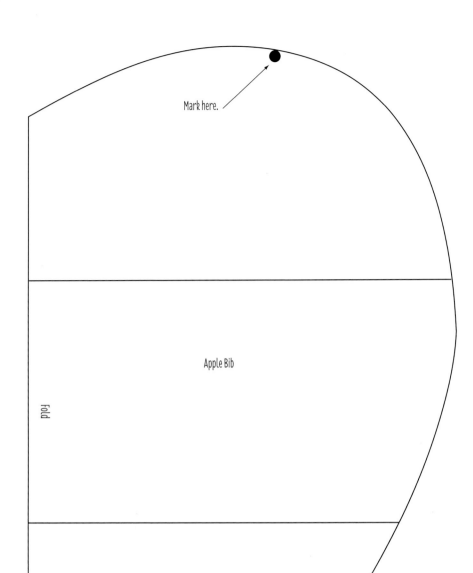

Mark here.

Apple Bib

Fold

fig. 1

Templates are actual size

Seed
Cut 2

fig. 2

Leaf

fig. 3

appliqué leaf and seeds

8 Using the template (**fig.** 2), trace two seeds onto the paper side of the fusible web, at least 1" (2.5 m) apart. Cut out each seed, leaving at least ⅛" (3 mm) margin around all edges.

9 Following the manufacturer's instructions, fuse web onto the wrong side of the brown seed fabric. Cut along the traced line. Fuse the seeds onto the bib front using the photo on page 60 as a reference.

10 Edgestitch the seed fabric to secure.

11 Create a leaf. Sew two green fabric scraps together and press open the seam. Place the leaf template (**fig.** 3) on the wrong side and trace, making sure that the seam is in the middle. Place the green backing fabric underneath the leaf, right sides together. Pin and sew along the traced line. Cut into the backing fabric (about 1½" [3.8 cm] wide opening) with a seam ripper or small scissors, being very careful not to cut the patchwork side. Turn the leaf right side out and press. Place this leaf piece on the bib where desired, and edgestitch into place using the photo on page 60 as a reference.

materials

Wool

○ Two scraps, each at least 13" × 13" (33 × 33 cm) square for main hat (or a fat quarter)

Assorted cotton print scraps

○ Ten scraps, each at least 3½" × 3½" (9 × 9 cm) square, for spikes

Print cotton

○ Two scraps, each at least 13" × 13" (33 x 33 cm) square for lining (or a fat quarter)

Six-strand embroidery floss

Cotton ribbon

○ Two 17" (43 cm) long strips

tools

Basic Quilting Tools (page 11)

Tailor's chalk

Freezer paper

Fabric marker

Point turner or chopstick

note

All seam allowances are ½" (1.3 cm), unless otherwise indicated.

Dino-Mite Hat

One young boy's love for dinosaurs—his name is Taihei—very much inspired me to make this hat. When it comes to Taihei, dinosaurs are the solution to everything in his life. If you know a boy or a girl who loves dinosaurs, make this hat to celebrate it. The hat is sized to fit an average toddler's head, and it is a pretty quick project—great for a little birthday gift or possibly a quick Halloween hat! Use cotton print fabric scraps or other fabrics to make fun spikes. The body of the hat is made with wool, but fleece or flannel can be great alternatives!

difficulty: ★ ★

finished size: 8½" × 10" (21.5 × 25.5 cm) (excluding spikes and ribbons)

make spikes

1 Trace the triangle template onto each print scrap (fig. 1). Cut along traced lines until you have five matching pairs of triangles from different fabrics (ten triangles in total).

2 Take one matching pair of the triangles created in Step 1. With the right sides together, place one on top of the other with edges aligned. Sew along two sides, pivoting at the corner. Repeat with the remaining four pairs of triangles.

3 For each spike, trim seam allowance around the pointy top, as shown in (fig. 2). Turn the piece right side out through the bottom opening, using a point turner tool or chopstick; press.

make hat

4 Trace the hat pattern (fig. 3) onto the matte side of freezer paper and cut out. Place this template on top of the wool and press lightly, so it temporarily attaches to the wool. Cut out the hat half, being careful not to cut into the template. Gently remove the freezer paper. Repeat for the second half of the hat. (If you are using fabric that has a right side and a wrong side, cut out one hat shape by ironing the template on the right side of the fabric and the other by ironing the template on the wrong side.)

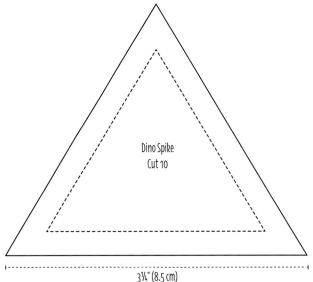

Dino Spike
Cut 10

3¼" (8.5 cm)
Seam allowance included.

fig. 1 Template is actual size

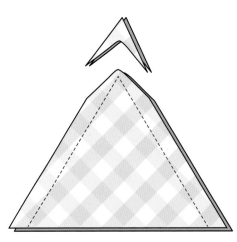

fig. 2 Template is actual size

5 With the right sides together, sew the dart in one hat piece and topstitch on the right side in a continuous line around the dart seam. Repeat for the other hat piece.

6 Machine-baste the raw-edged base of the spikes to the top edge of one hat piece. Position the first one about ½" (1.3 cm) away from the front of the hat. Position the second spike next to the first one, making sure there is no gap between the spikes. Machine-baste. Repeat until you have basted all five spikes.

7 With the right sides together, sew the two hat pieces together along the top edge. Reduce bulkiness by pressing the dart seam allowance on each half in opposite directions.

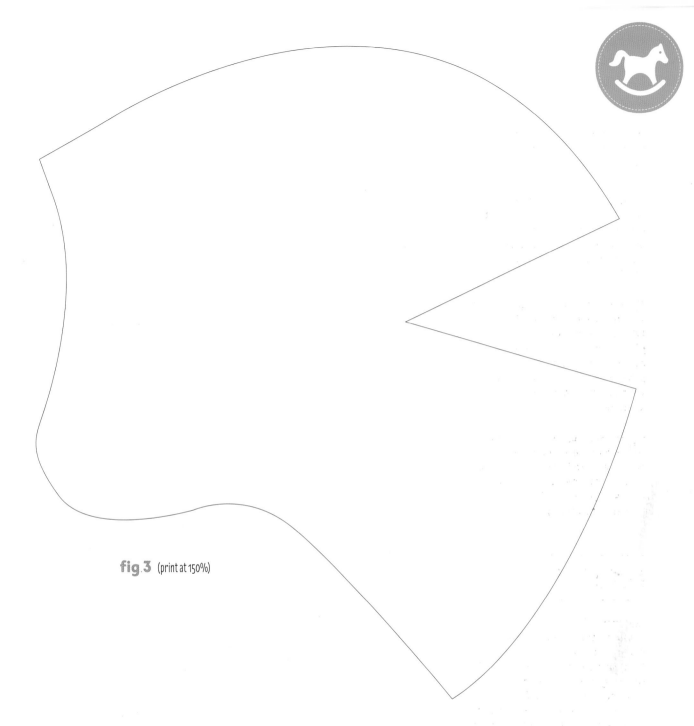

fig.3 (print at 150%)

8 At the bottom edges of the hat, baste a ribbon with the wrong side of the ribbon up as you are sewing. At the other end of the ribbon strip, fold under twice (½" [1.3 cm]) and sew very close to the folded edge to secure.

9 Repeat Steps 4–7 to make a lining (omitting the spikes).

10 With the right sides together, sew the lining and exterior hat together, making sure that the ribbon straps are inside, free of the seam. Leave an opening about 2½" (6.5 cm) at the base of the hat and turn the hat right side out through the opening. Slipstitch the opening closed.

11 If desired, add running stitches along the bottom edge of the hat or machine topstitch for a finished look.

materials

Assorted cotton print and solid scraps for 16 book blocks, as follows *(measurements are for a single book block; you will need 16 sets of each)*:

○ Book cover: 5" × 6¼" (12.7 × 16 cm)
○ Book sashing: 2" × 6¼" (5 × 16 cm) (each side); 1½" × 8¼" (4 × 21 cm) (top and bottom)
○ Book spine: 1⅛" × 6¼" (3 × 16 cm)
○ Corners and page accents: assorted small scraps

Cotton print

○ Thirty-two 1¼" × 8¼" (3.2 × 21 cm) strips for top and bottom borders of each block
○ Thirty-two 1¼" × 9¾" (3.2 × 25 cm) strips for side borders each block (¾ yd (68.5 cm) of this fabric will suffice).

Cotton solid

○ Twenty-four 1½" × 9¾" (3.2 × 25 cm) strips for sashing between blocks (½ yd (45.5 cm) of this fabric will suffice).

Assorted cotton prints to contrast with cotton solid above

○ Nine 1½" (3.2 cm) squares for blocks between sashing

Cotton print

○ Two 4¼" × 40½" (11 × 103 cm) strips for large borders at top and bottom edges
○ Two 4¼" × 48" (11 × 122 cm) strips for large borders at side edges. (This can be the same fabric joined. I made these borders by joining two fabric strips. In this case, ¾ yd (68.5 cm) is needed.)

Materials continued on next page.

Books-for-Baby Quilt

I love this quilt because a little one will enjoy coming up with stories about each and every book, and you will have fun making sixteen unique book blocks for a 48" × 48" (122 × 122 cm) baby quilt. Use a wide variety of playful fabric prints—animals, candies, vehicles, flowers—everything your little one is crazy about! The scrappiness is balanced by the uniform border around all the book squares and the solid sashing. So go ahead, choose whatever fabrics you want to use!

difficulty: ★ ★ ★
finished size: 48" × 48" (122 × 122 cm)

Cotton print

○ One 52" × 52" (132 × 132 cm) square for quilt backing. (This can be joined in any way desired. If it is made with just one cotton print; you'll need 3 yd (274.5 cm) of cotton print. If you choose a scattered rather than a uniform print, the joins will be less obvious.)

Cotton solid

○ Twelve 20" × 3¾" (51 × 9.5 cm) strips for binding tape

Cotton batting

○ One 52" × 52" (132 × 132 cm) square

tools

Basic Quilting Tools (page 11)

Quilting adhesive spray

16 sheets of 8½" × 11" (21.5 × 28 cm) standard copy paper

Washi tape or masking tape *(optional)*

note

All seam allowances are ¼" (6 mm), unless otherwise indicated.

assemble quilt top

1 Photocopy the provided template (fig. 1) eight times. Make sure that the printed block measures 7¾" (19.5 cm) square. Flip the template horizontally and photocopy eight more blocks. You should have eight book block templates opening on the right and eight book block templates opening on the left.

2 Cut the templates along the line where indicated. You will complete these two sections separately, then sew them together to finish each single book block.

3 Referring to the paper-piecing method (page 19), foundation-piece both segments of these sixteen blocks. Be sure to keep together each set that uses the same book sashing fabric. When each section is complete, sew the top and bottom segments, right sides together, along the top of the block.

4 Attach border strips to each book block. With the right sides together, sew the shorter border strips to the top and bottom edges of the block; press toward the border. Sew border strips to side edges of the block and press toward the border.

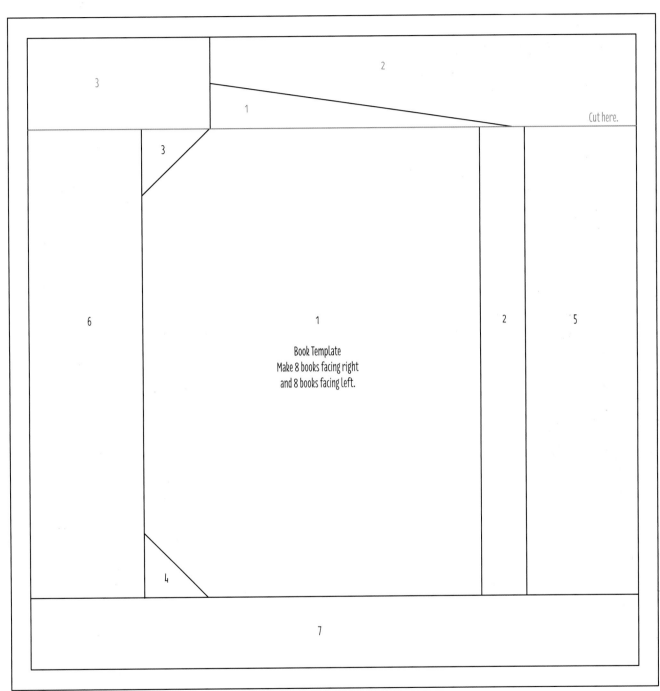

3

2

1

Cut here.

3

6

1

2

5

Book Template
Make 8 books facing right
and 8 books facing left.

4

7

fig. 1 (print at 118%)

5 Decide placement of the book blocks. It might be fun to place them so that no two blocks next to each other face the same direction, as shown on page 68. Arrange four blocks horizontally from left to right for the first column.

6 Starting with the bottom of the first block and ending with the top of the last block in the column, join the blocks in the first column with sashing. Press seams toward the sashing. Repeat the same process to create three more columns.

7 Create three long strips of sashing, consisting of four short solid strips alternately joined by three 1½" (3.8 cm) squares sewn between each short strip. Start and finish with a short solid strip. Press seams toward the sashing.

8 Sew columns together with sashing strips between each column. Pin carefully before sewing to ensure that the small squares in the sashing fit perfectly between the book block sashing strips. Press the seams of the sashing where columns meet toward the sashing.

9 Sew shorter large borders to the sides of the quilt top. Press seams toward the border. Sew long large borders to the top and bottom edges of the quilt top to complete your quilt top. Press.

quilt and bind

10 Place the quilt backing print on a large flat space, wrong side up. Tape the edges of the backing to the flat surface to straighten the fabric. Apply adhesive spray thoroughly to one half of the backing and gently place one half of the cotton batting on top. Smooth the batting to make sure it adheres well. Complete by lifting the unattached half of the batting and apply spray to the remaining half of the backing; adhere batting. Remove tape from quilt backing.

11 Using the method from Step 10, attach the quilt top to the batting.

12 Machine- or hand-quilt as desired. I machine-quilted my quilt by stitching around each book, border, and each small brown square.

13 Using the double-fold binding tape method (page 27), join binding strips to create an approximately 200" (255 cm) long tape.

14 Using ½" (1.3 cm) seam allowance, sew the binding tape around all the edges of the quilt. You could either (a) start with a folded short edge and overwrap the end or (b) leave approximately 5" (12.5 cm) unsewn at the beginning and then sew this edge to the end of the binding tape for less bulkiness. (See Binding, page 26.)

15 Pin the binding tape in place on the back of the quilt. Make sure that machine stitching from the front of the quilt is completely covered by the folded edge of the tape. With the quilt top facing up, edgestitch the binding tape to complete attaching the tape.

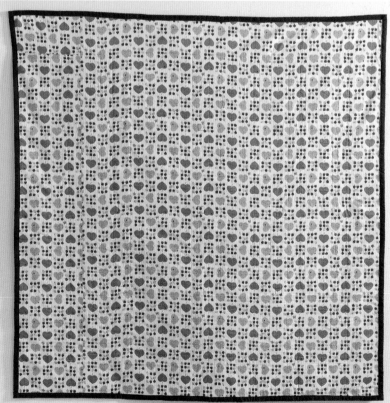

for the Home

materials

Linen
- ○ Two 7½" × 6½" (19 × 16.5 cm) rectangles for pockets
- ○ Two 5¾" × 6½" (14.5 × 16.5 cm) rectangles for exterior sides
- ○ One 9" × 6½" (23 × 16.5) rectangle for bottom

Assorted cotton prints
- ○ Many rectangles in various lengths, 1½" (3.8 cm) wide for front and back exterior

Cotton print
- ○ Two 9" × 5¾" (23 × 14.5 cm) rectangles for front and back lining
- ○ Two 6½" × 5¾" (16.5 × 14.5 cm) rectangles for side lining
- ○ One 9½" × 7½" (24 × 19 cm) rectangle for base lining

Heavyweight interfacing or chipboard
- ○ Two 7⅞" × 4⅞" (20 × 12.25 cm) rectangles for front and back
- ○ Two 5⅞" × 4⅞" (14.75 × 12.25 cm) rectangles for sides
- ○ One 7⅞" × 5⅞" (20 × 14.75 cm) rectangle for base

Paper for foundation piecing
- ○ Two 5½" × 9" (14 × 23 cm) rectangles

Lightweight interfacing
- ○ One 7⅞" × 5⅞" (20 × 14.75 cm) rectangle for base

tools

Basic Quilting Tools (page 11)
Fabric glue stick
Marking pen
Rotary cutter
Acrylic ruler
Craft adhesive spray

note

All seam allowances are ¼" (6 mm), unless otherwise indicated.

My Scrappy Box

In this project, I use a fabric scrap that is just a little over 1½" (3.8 cm) wide, and turn it into a big star! Many of the fabric scraps for this project came from my scrappy fabric bin, reminding me that keeping small fabric scraps is a good habit that can give great results. I hope your saved scraps will do the same for you!

difficulty: ★ ★ ★

finished size: 8" (20.5 cm) wide × 5" (12.5 cm) high × 6" (15 cm) deep

make patchwork panels

1 Arrange your small rectangular scraps into five rows. For each row, sew together the short edges of each piece until the strip is about 9" (23 cm) long. Press open seams. You should now have five 1½" × 9" (3.8 x 23 cm) strips.

2 Using a marking pen or pencil, draw lines on one of the foundation paper rectangles. Draw a line parallel to one long edge that is 1¼" (3.2 cm) from the edge. Next, draw another line parallel to the first that is 1" (2.5 cm) from the first line. Repeat this two more times, so that you have a foundation paper with four lines spaced 1" (2.5 cm) apart and two lines 1¼" (3.2 cm) from the top and bottom long edges of the paper.

3 Choose the patchwork strip that will be at the top of your box and dab some fabric glue on the wrong side. Attach this strip on the wrong side (the side without drawn lines) of the paper for foundation piecing, with its top long edge aligned with one long edge of the paper.

4 Place the second-to-top patchwork strip on top of the first patchwork strip with the right sides together, bottom edge aligned with the top edge of the first patchwork strip. Pin in place.

5 Turn the paper and sew along the line closest to the top edge. By doing this, you are sewing the two patchwork strips together. Turn

the paper and press the second patchwork strip down. Repeat the same process for three more strips. After all five strips are sewn together onto the paper, turn the paper and cut off the excess fabric using a ruler and a rotary cutter. The paper will serve as interfacing, so keep the paper on. Repeat Steps 1 to 6 to create a second patchwork panel. Set aside.

6 Sew lining to the front patchwork panel, right sides together, leaving the bottom edge

{ **tip** }

You can also piece the patchwork rows together to create patchwork front and back panels, each measuring 6½" x 9" (16.5 x 23 cm), and add a panel of interfacing to the wrong side of the fabric.

open. Clip the top two corners and turn right side out; press. Repeat the same process for the back patchwork panel.

make pocketed side panels

7 Fold one of the 7½" × 6½" (19 × 16.5 cm) linen pieces in half widthwise to create a pocket and

press. Place this piece onto one of the 5¾" × 6½" (14.5 × 16.5 cm) linen side panel pieces, with raw edges aligned with the side and bottom edges of the side panels. Edgestitch so the stitching will be hidden in construction seam allowances.

8 Repeat Step 7 to create another pocket and side panel piece.

9 With the right sides together, attach lining to one linen side panel, stitching all edges together except the bottom edge. Use ½" (1.3 cm) seam allowances for

the sides and a ¼" (6 mm) seam allowance for the top edge. Trim the ½" (1.3 cm) seam allowances on the sides to ¼" (6 mm). There will be ½" (1.3 cm) overlapping with the bottom of the side panel, which will be sewn as well. Clip the top corners and turn right side out. Press.

10 Repeat Step 9 for the other side panel.

assemble box

11 Using a marking pen, draw a line on the wrong side of the linen rectangle for the box base, ½" (1.3 cm) from the lower edge.

12 Sew the bottom edge of one patchwork panel to the long edge of the linen base piece with right sides together, leaving the lining edge free. Sew the second patchwork panel's bottom edge to the other long edge of the linen piece, again leaving the lining edge free. Press open seams.

13 On the right side of the linen base piece in Step 11, place one side piece with the linen side on top and with its bottom edge aligned with one short edge of the linen section. Turn the lining piece up so that you will sew only the linen exterior of the side piece to the base. (You'll add interfacing from the opening later, so do not sew this hole shut.) Sew along the line you drew using a ½" (1.3 cm) seam allowance. Repeat for the other side piece so that both side pieces are attached to the linen base piece.

14 Turn the patchwork sides inside out. All four side

pieces are attached to the linen base piece, each of them with an open bottom lining edge. Insert 5⅞" × 4⅞" (14.75 × 12.25 cm) heavyweight interfacing into each panel opening. Fuse lightweight interfacing to the inside base, underneath the overlapping lining seam allowances.

15 Handstitch (ladder stitch) panels together on the lining side, one at a time (fig. 1).

16 Spray adhesive thoroughly on the wrong side of the lining piece for the base. Attach the interfacing for the base in the middle. Carefully fold all corners inward and adhere each edge to the back of the base, interfacing one by one (fig. 2).

17 Now, spray adhesive thoroughly again on the wrong side of the base and carefully insert inside the basket to adhere to the very bottom. Press firmly to secure.

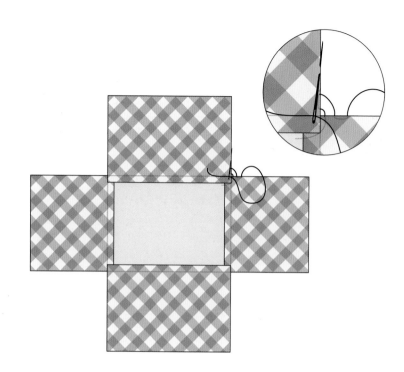

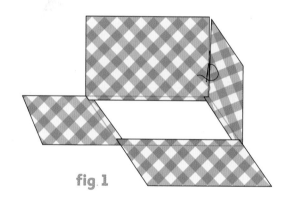

fig. 1

fig. 2

materials

Assorted cotton solids
○ Nine scraps of various colors, each at least 6" × 6" (15 × 15 cm) for flower center parts

Assorted cotton prints
○ Nine different fat quarters for flower middle parts
○ Nine different fat quarters for flower outermost parts

Dark green cotton solid
○ Eighteen scraps, each at least 3" × 10" (7.5 × 25.5 cm) for dark leaf halves

Light green cotton solid
○ Ten scraps, each at least 3" × 10" (7.5 × 25.5 cm) for light leaf halves

Assorted green cotton prints
○ Eight scraps, each at least 3" × 10" (7.5 × 25.5 cm) for light leaf halves

White cotton solid
○ 2 yd (183 cm) for flower and leaf blocks
○ Six 4" × 18" (10 × 45.5 cm) rectangles for white blocks between flowers in a row
○ Two 3¼" × 45" (8.5 × 114.5 cm) strips for white sashing between rows
○ Two 2½" × 58" (6.5 × 147.5 cm) strips for white sashing beside columns
○ Two 2½" × 48½" (6.5 × 123 cm) strips for white sashing above the top row and below the bottom row

Assorted cotton solids and prints
○ Total of 4 yd (366 cm) for making 76½" × 62½" (194.5 × 159 cm) quilt backing

Materials continued on next page.

Swedish Bloom– Time Lap Quilt

This quilt was inspired by a traditional Swedish flower design. I love the strong presence of the design, created with just a simple shape and a few colors. It's so beautiful and eye-pleasing. In this quilt, there is a little twist to add an element of fun to the process of making each block: each of the quilt's nine flowers features a different colorway. The border and the binding tape are made of scraps to add some sass to the simple design.

difficulty: ★★★★
finished size: 58½" × 71½" (148.5 × 182 cm)

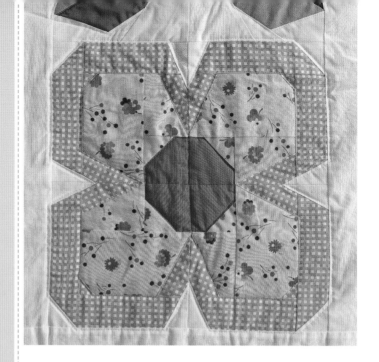

Assorted cotton prints

○ Several different 5¼" (13.5 cm) wide rectangles for making:

    ○ Two 58½" × 5¼" (148.5 × 13.5 cm) strips for top and bottom borders

    ○ Two 72½" × 5¼" (183 × 13.5 cm) strips for right and left side borders

Assorted cotton solids and prints

○ Several different 2¾" (7 cm) wide strips, sufficient to create two 59½" (151 cm) and two 72½" (184 cm) long double binding tapes

45 sheets of 8.5" × 11" (21.5 × 28 cm) copy paper

3 yd (274.5 cm) lightweight fusible quilt batting

tools

Basic Quilting Tools (page 11)
Fabric glue stick
Quilting adhesive spray
Washi tape or masking tape
Walking foot or darning foot

note

All seam allowances are ¼" (6 mm), unless otherwise indicated.

assemble blocks

1 Photocopy the petal template {fig. 1} onto 36 sheets of paper. You will need 4 photocopies of this template to complete one flower. Photocopy the leaves templates {fig. 2, page 86} onto 9 sheets. Cut out each of the templates with a ¼" (6 mm) seam allowance around all edges.

2 Paper-piece fabric onto all the printouts (see page 19). You will start by dabbing a bit of glue on the wrong side of the paper in the area with number "1." Attach a piece of fabric to it, leaving at least ¼" (6 mm) seam allowances around all edges. For the flowers, start with a solid, which will be in the center of the flower. Then piece in order from 1–12. Repeat to create 9 sets of a flower consisting of 4 templates. Using the same method, complete 18 leaves with green fabrics. After pressing, carefully remove all the paper by peeling off gently.

3 Assemble the flower using the construction template on page 87 {fig 3}.

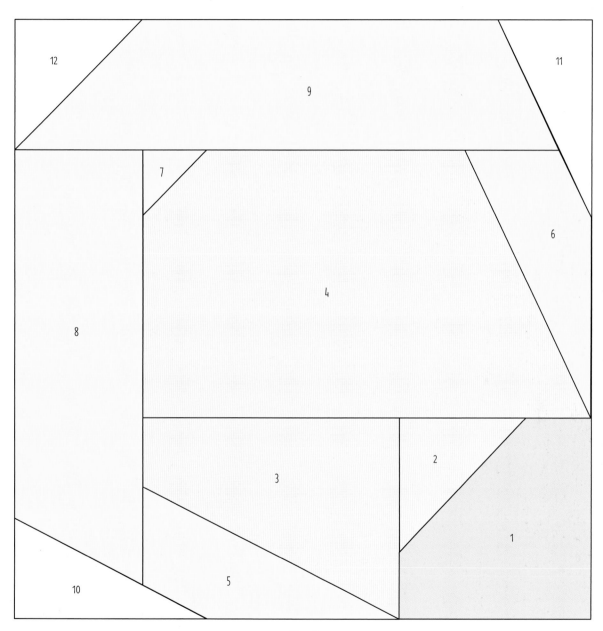

fig. 1

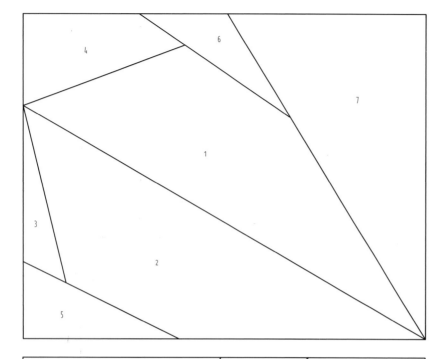

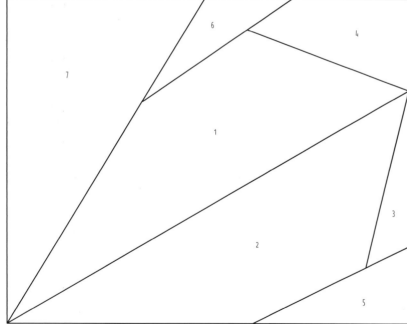

fig. 2 (print at 143%)

4 Take one set of leaves (two blocks) and sew them together with the right sides together. Press seam open. Sew these leaves to the flower using the constrution template on the facing page (**fig. 3**). Repeat the same process for the remaining pieces to complete a set of 9 flowers with leaves.

5 Decide the placement of the blocks. It might be fun to invert some of the blocks.

6 Create one row by adding sashing between the first and the second flower sets, and between the second and the third flower sets, separating each flower set in the row by about 3½" (9 cm) (the width of sashing in between). Repeat to complete the remaining two rows.

7 Sew sashing between each row. Then sew sashing to the right and left edges and then to the top and bottom edges. Set aside.

quilt and attach borders

8 Make a backing that is at least 76½" × 62½" (194.5 × 159 cm). You can use a single print or solid, or combine a few different prints by sewing them together. This will extend beyond the finished quilt top by a few inches all around. Place this backing on a flat surface (such as a wooden floor or tabletop), wrong side up. Tape all edges to the surface to make sure that the backing is completely straight and flat and won't slip. Spray adhesive

fig. 3

thoroughly on the backing, and place batting carefully on top of it, fusible side up. Smooth over to attach well.

9 Remove tape from backing. Now carefully place the quilt top right in the middle of the batting, smooth, and fuse according to manufacturer's directions. Set this aside.

10 Make four borders that are each 5¼" (13.5 cm) wide. You can use a single print or combine a few different prints. Start with the top and bottom borders: once each border is at least 58½" (148.5 cm) long, sew to the quilt top through the batting and backing layers, right sides together. Open out the border, press, and topstitch close to the seam lines. Then quilt close to the other long raw edges through the quilt layers. Trim excess if the border is longer than the top and bottom edges of the quilt top. Repeat the same process to sew side borders to the quilt top: left and right borders should measure at least 71½" (182 cm) each. This is the easiest way to attach the borders, but you can also sew all four borders in a log cabin style pattern. See the finished quilt on the facing page. Borders are sewn in the following order: bottom, to left side, to top, to right side.

11 Quilt as desired. My method was to: (1) quilt around flowers and leaves using white thread, (2) quilt around the flower center and stitch in the ditch on the seams in the flower center using thread that matches the color of the flower center, (3) quilt close to the seams between the middle flower to the outer flower, and 4) stitch in the ditch on the seam between each leaf using green thread.

bind the quilt edges

12 Make four double binding tapes. You can use one print/solid or make it scrappy. (See page 27, double binding tapes.) Attach binding tapes to the top and bottom edges of the quilt first, with ½" (1.3 cm) seam allowances. Pin the folded edge of the binding tape onto the backing and sew very close to the edge of the binding tape, with the front side of the quilt facing up. When you are sewing through the layers, make sure your stitches are catching the binding tape on the back. Trim excess. (You can leave the short edges of the binding raw.) Attach binding tapes to the side edges in the same manner. This time you want to make sure the binding tapes are long enough, so that you'll have at least ¾" (2 cm) extra on top and bottom edges; wrap around the corners before stitching to the ends.

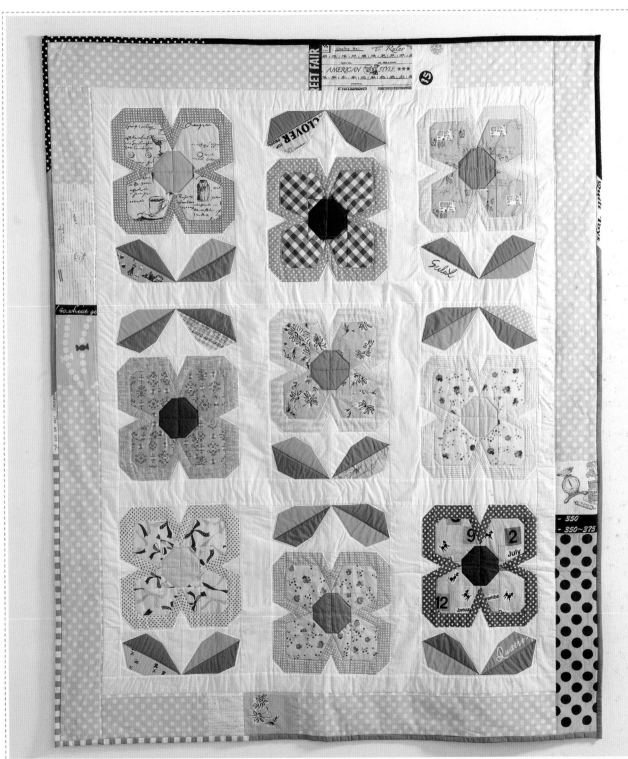

materials

Linen
- One 24½" × 31½" (62 × 80 cm) rectangle for front base
- Two scraps measuring at least 2½" × 3½" (6.5 × 9 cm) for pencil wooden parts

Assorted cotton prints
- Eight scraps measuring at least 4½" × 5½" (11.5 × 14 cm) for eight envelopes
- Two scraps measuring at least 4½" × 3½" (11.5 × 9 cm) for two pencil bodies

Assorted cotton solids
- Nine scraps measuring at least 10" × 10" (25.5 × 25.5 cm) for envelope backgrounds
- Eight scraps measuring at least 8" × 8" (20.5 × 20.5 cm) for envelopes
- Two scraps measuring at least 2" × 2" (5 × 5 cm) for pencil tops

Cotton print
- ½ yd (45.5 cm) for binding tape

Cotton print
- One 24½" × 31½" (62 × 80 cm) rectangle for backing

Cotton or linen print
- Three 20½" × 7½" (52 × 19 cm) rectangles for pocket backing

Cotton batting
- One 24½" × 31½" (62 × 80 cm) rectangle

Three 7" (18 cm) long ribbons for hangers

Nine papers (one paper for each of eight envelopes, one paper for two pencil blocks) for paper-piecing and to be left on as a stabilizer

Materials continued on next page.

You've-Got-Mail Wall Pocket

This is a fun wall pocket for organizing mail and related things like pens, pencils, and stationery. Make as many or as few pockets as you wish, to satisfy your organizing needs. You might want to match up the number of envelope pockets with the members of your family, labeling each pocket with a name. For larger mail, you can combine two envelope blocks into a single pocket.

difficulty: ★ ★ ★
finished size: 20½" × 27½" (52 × 70 cm)

tools

Basic Quilting Tools (page 11)
Rotary cutter
Acrylic ruler
Quilting adhesive spray
Washi tape or masking tape
Fabric glue

note

All seam allowances are ½" (1.3 cm),
unless otherwise indicated.

paper-piece blocks

1 Enlarge the envelope and pencil
templates (fig. 1, page 93, and
fig. 2, page 95). Both templates
call for 6½" (16.5 cm) high blocks
without seam allowances. The pencil
block template is 3¼" (8.5 cm), so
when two pencils are joined, they
match the 6½" width (16.5 cm) of
the envelope block. You will need
eight papers with an envelope block
printed (one block per paper) and
one paper with two pencil blocks
printed.

2 Using the paper-piecing
method (page 19), complete
eight envelopes and two pencils,
trimming interior block seams to
¼" (6 mm). Blocks should be same
size as template plus ½" (1.3 cm)
seam allowance (in accordance with
instructions) on all sides. When you
are done paper-piecing, use a rotary
cutter and an acrylic ruler to trim
excess fabric. Leave the paper on as
a stabilizer.

3 Place two pencil blocks next to
each other with one pointing up
and the other pointing down. Place
one on top of the other, with one
long edge matching. Sew along the
edge so that you will have a block of

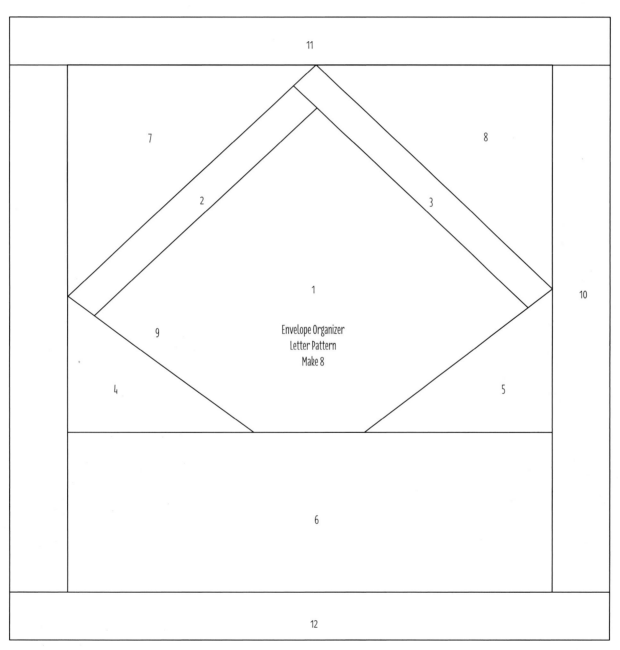

fig. 1 Template is actual size

two pencils next to each other, with a border around it as shown in the photograph above.

4 Decide on the placement of the blocks, creating three rows of three blocks each. (See photo of finished project on page 90 for placement ideas.)

5 To make the first horizontal row of three blocks, sew the left block to the middle block along the left side, and then the right block to the middle block along the right side. Press. With the right sides together, place the print for pocket backing on top of the row and sew along both long edges (top and bottom). Press open seams. Trim corners. Turn the piece right side out from the opening and press. Repeat the same process for the remaining two rows. Set aside.

make a wall pocket base

6 Sandwich batting between the linen and the print backing, with wrong sides facing the batting. Spray adhesive thoroughly on the wrong sides of the linen and the print to temporarily attach them to the batting. Smooth to make sure there are no wrinkles.

7 Quilt as desired. I quilted so that each line of diagonal stitching was spaced about 1½" (3.8 cm) apart.

8 Once the piece is quilted, trim the excess material so the final piece measures 20½" × 27½" (52 × 70 cm).

9 Place the first row of envelope blocks so that the top edge of the row is 3" (7.5 cm) from the top edge of the quilted linen and pin in place. Sew very close to the bottom edge on the pocket all the way from the right edge to the left. If you wish to divide the pocket into three sections with the blocks, stitch in the ditch of the seam lines that are connecting the middle block to the right block, as well as to the left block. Using a thread color that matches the background of the middle block will make the stitching less visible.

10 Place two more rows on the base so that there is about 2¼" (5.5 cm) between the bottom edge of the top row to the top edge of the second row. The same spacing is also used between the second and the third rows.

11 Sew the second and the third rows in the same manner you sewed the first row to the base. It might be interesting to have one or two pockets that are larger than others. I divided the first two rows into three pockets. As for the third row, there is no division between two envelope blocks, in order to allow for larger pieces of mail. There is a division between two pencils to make two narrow pockets for pencils.

12 Machine-baste three ribbons at the top edge of the base on the back. Place one ribbon in the middle of the top edge: have the two short edges align with the top edge, pin in place, and sew very close to the short edges. Sew two other ribbons close to corners at the top edge, making sure to leave at least ½" (1.3 cm) spacing from each side edge for attaching a binding tape.

13 Make a double-fold binding tape. Cut out 3¾" (9.5 cm) wide bias strips from the fabric for a binding tape. Sew the short edges together to create one strip that is at least 104" (264 cm) long. Fold in half lengthwise with right sides together and press. Start somewhere in the middle on one edge, and leave about 5" (12.5 cm) without sewing. Stop about 5" (12.5 cm) from the short edge of the binding tape where you started and backstitch. Draw a line where the binding tape overlaps ½" (1.3 cm) and trim the excess. Use a ¼" (6 mm) seam allowance to sew together the short edges. Finish sewing the binding to the wall organizer. (See Binding, page 26.)

14 Handstitch to finish attaching binding tape to the back. Next, tack the ribbons to the binding so that the wall pocket will hang straight when mounted.

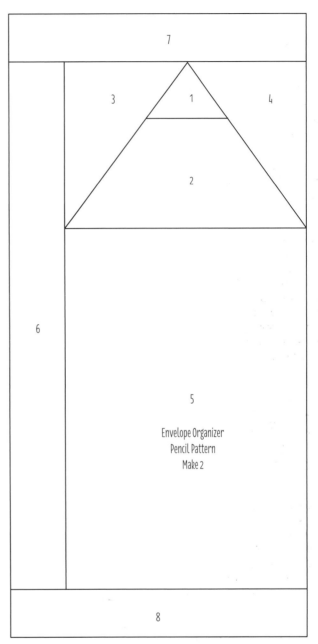

fig. 2 Template is actual size

materials

Five assorted cotton prints
○ Each at least ⅛ yd for patchwork pieces
(4½" × 5½" or 11.5 × 14 cm)

Cotton print
○ Two 20" × 2¼" (51 × 5.5 cm) strips
(either bias or nonbias is fine) for
double-fold binding tape

Cotton solid
○ One scrap, at least 5" × 5" (12.5 × 12.5 cm)
square for middle part of patchwork

Cotton print
○ One 11" × 11" (28 × 28 cm) square for
backing

Insulated batting
○ One 11" × 11" (28 × 28 cm) square

tools

Basic Quilting Tools (page 11)

One sheet of 8½" × 11" (21.5 × 28 cm)
copy paper

Quilting adhesive spray

Walking foot *(optional)*

note

All seam allowances are ¼" (6 mm),
unless otherwise indicated.

Happy Hexagon Trivet

This is a quick project that can be used as a trivet, mug rug, potholder, or just a surface to place a nice object on, such as a teapot or a vase with flowers! It is foundation pieced, so you'll be sewing pieces onto a paper in order just like a log cabin pattern. Your hexagon top will be done before you know it. I made mine using six different fabrics, but you can experiment with a variety of fabric combinations. Maybe add kitchen-themed embroidery, or a sweet embroidered message in the center? Lots of possibilities!

difficulty: ★ ★

finished size: 9½" (24 cm) (from one corner to the other side of a corner)

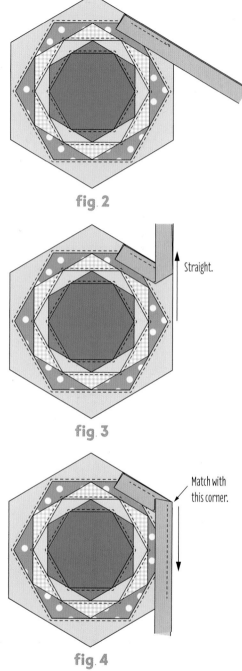

fig. 2

fig. 3

Straight.

fig. 4

Match with this corner.

assemble trivet

1 Print out **Fig. 1** onto a piece of paper. Make sure that the distance from one outermost edge to the other outermost edge measures 7¾" (19.5 cm).

2 Glue the wrong side of the fabric piece you want to use for the #1 area onto the center back of the paper template. Referring to the paper-piecing method (page 19), foundation-piece the hexagon, beginning by piecing the #2 pieces to the #1 center. After sewing each piece, trim the seam allowance to ¼" (6 mm) and press to one side toward the outside of the hexagon. Continue to paper-piece each row of the hexagon according to **Fig. 1** until all rows are pieced. Gently remove the paper from the back.

3 Apply adhesive spray thoroughly to the back of the patchwork hexagon and place it on top of the batting. Smooth to secure. Attach backing onto the back of the batting, using the spray.

4 Quilt as desired. (If you have a walking foot, I recommend you use it, in order to keep the patchwork nice.) I machine-quilted by outlining the hexagons. Once quilting is done, cut off the excess batting and backing. Set aside.

5 Using a double-fold binding tape method (described on page 27), make a binding tape by sewing the short ends of the two 20" × 2¼" (51 × 5.5 cm) long strips together. With the wrong sides together, fold ¼" (6 mm) from one short edge toward wrong side and iron to press. Then, with wrong sides together,

fold the strip in half lengthwise: press.

6 Machine-stitch the right side of the binding, starting with the folded end described in Step 5 and raw edges together, to the

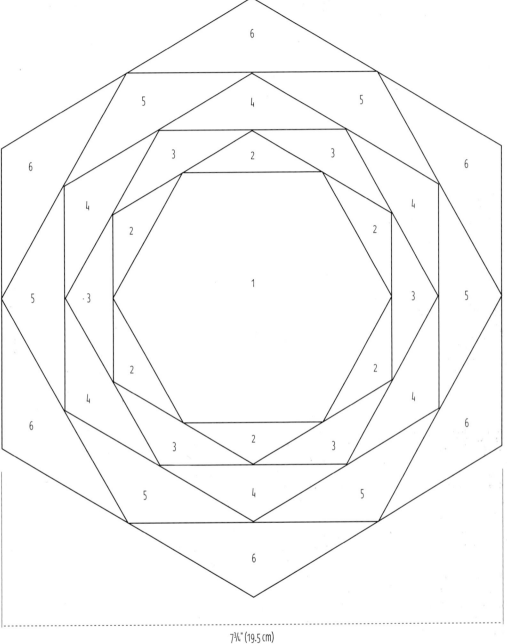

7¾" (19.5 cm)

fig. 1 (print at 143%)

hexagon right side. As you sew the binding, stop and backstitch at ¼" (6 mm) before you reach each corner. Remove the hexagon trivet from the sewing machine, and wrap binding tape as illustrated (figs. 2–4). Once you place the tape onto the hexagon, start sewing from the very edge. When you reach the place where you started, sew until ¼" (6 mm) of the binding tape is overwrapping. Trim excess.

7 Handstitch on the back to finish attaching the binding tape.

for Going Places

materials

Medium to heavy weight fabric, such as home décor fabric or linen
- ○ Two 15" × 14¼" (38 × 36 cm) rectangles for front and back exteriors
- ○ Two 18" × 14¼" (45.5 × 36 cm) rectangles for side exteriors
- ○ One 15" × 9" (38 × 23 cm) rectangle for bottom exterior
- ○ One 6¾" × 5½" (17 × 14 cm) for pocket backing

Cotton print
- ○ Two 32½" × 12½" (82.5 × 31.5 cm) rectangles for drawstring cover

Recycled lightweight plastic tablecloth or equivalent, such as laminated fabric or oil cloth
- ○ Two 15" × 14¼" (38 × 36 cm) rectangles for front and back interiors
- ○ Two 18" × 14¼" (45.5 × 36 cm) rectangles for side interiors
- ○ One 15" × 9" (38 × 23 cm) rectangle for base interior

Assorted cotton prints
- ○ Five rectangles, each measuring 6¾" × 1½" (17 × 3.8 cm)

Cording
- ○ Two 67½" (171.5 cm) pieces for drawstring

Cotton webbing
- ○ Two 43" (109 cm) long strips for handles

tools

Basic Quilting Tools (page 11)

Fabric marker

Fabric glue

Pinking shears

note

All seam allowances are ¼" (6 mm), unless otherwise indicated.

Piece-of-Cake Shopping Bag

Go eco with this shopping bag! The bag fits perfectly into a grocery store basket. Place the bag's drawstring cover over the edges of the basket and place your groceries into the bag. When you have paid for your groceries, simply pull the drawstring closed, grab the handles, and go! The interior of the bag is lined with a recycled plastic tablecloth, so you can easily wipe up if anything spills inside the bag. The patchwork pocket is the icing on the cake!

difficulty: ★ ★

finished size: 12½" H × 14½" W × 8½" D (bottom) (31.5 × 37 × 21.5 cm), 17½" D (top) (44.5 cm)

make a pocket

1 Arrange the five 6¾" × 1½" (17 x 3.8 cm) rectangular strips in a pleasing order, using the photo at right as a guide. Sew strips together along the long edges with right sides together, until a 6¾" x 5½" (17 x 14 cm) is formed. (Trim if necessary to arrive at this final measurement.)

2 Place the linen rectangle for pocket backing on top of the patchwork panel, with right sides together. Pin in place and sew along top and bottom edges.

3 Turn right side out through side opening and press. Topstitch top and bottom edges. Use an erasable fabric marker to mark the center point at the top and bottom edges of the pocket on the right side.

4 Fold one of the front exterior rectangle pieces in half lengthwise lightly to make a crease in the middle. Place the wrong side of the pocket piece onto the right side of the rectangle, aligning the pocket and rectangle pieces in the center. The bottom edge of the pocket should measure 2¾" (7 cm) from the bottom of the rectangle. Make sure that the marks on the pocket are aligned with the crease on the front exterior panel. Pin in place and sew both short side edges and the bottom edge using a ⅛" (3 mm) seam allowance.

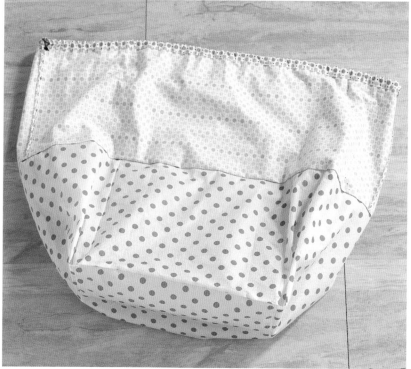

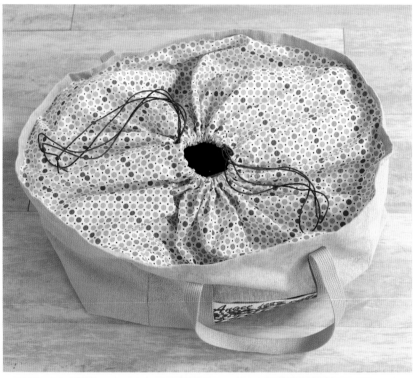

assemble exterior and interior bags

5 Loop one handle onto the front exterior panel so that the two ends are aligned with the bottom edge, and cover ¼" (6 mm) of the pocket along both edges. Make sure the handle is not twisted. Gluing the underside of the handle to the front panel with fabric glue will help to keep it in place before stitching.

6 Measure 11" (28 cm) from the bottom edge of each handle piece and mark with the fabric marker. You will now sew these handles onto the front exterior by sewing close to the edge on each side of the handle until you reach the mark. Then, sew across to the other side and stitch down to the short bottom edge. Repeat this for the other side of the handle.

7 Repeat Steps 5–6 for the back exterior panel.

8 Place one rectangle for the side exterior panel on top of the front exterior panel, with right sides together and the right edges aligned. Sew along the right edge. Repeat the same process to sew another side piece to the other short edge of the front exterior panel. Then, sew the back exterior panel to one of the side panels so that four pieces are now sewn together in one long piece.

9 At the bottom edge of the side panel, mark 4½" (11.5 cm) from each seam. You will have two marks that are 8½" (21.5 cm) apart from each other (fig. 1). The short edge of this should be 8½" (21.5 cm) long

at the bottom, so bring the mark to the seam close to it, making a fold on the back. Using a ⅛" (3 mm) seam allowance, sew along the bottom edge to keep the fold in place (fig. 2). Repeat the same process for the other marked point.

10 Align the two remaining short edges of the bag piece, with right sides together, and sew along the edge so that it forms a loop. Repeat Step 9 (tuck making) for the other side panel.

11 Sew the exterior base piece to the loop, right sides together, one edge at a time. Pin as necessary.

12 Assemble an interior bag in the same way you assembled the exterior bag, except for the attachment of a pocket and handles.

13 At the top edge of the exterior bag, make a ¾" (2 cm) wide double fold with the wrong sides together. Press.

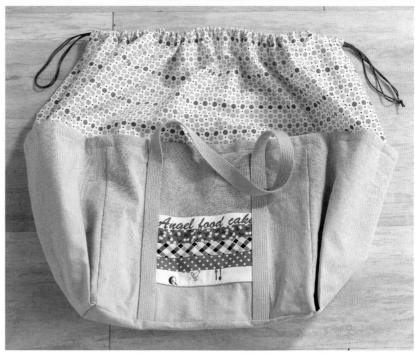

complete bag

14 Make a drawstring cover. Take the two rectangles for the cover, and with wrong sides together sew along both short edges, leaving 2" (5 cm) open from the top edge. Pink these seam allowances to protect them from fraying.

15 Press open seam. Make sure to also press the top part that is not sewn. With wrong sides

together, fold ¼" (6 mm) from the top edge all the way around the drawstring cover. Then fold again ¾" (2 cm). Press and sew very close to the fold.

16 Place the drawstring cover inside the interior bag. (The right side of the bag and the wrong side of the cover should face each other.) Use clips to hold in place. Align top edges and sew all the way along the edge.

17 Place the piece from Step 16 inside the exterior bag, with the wrong sides of each bag together. Cover the top edge of the lining completely, so that the top edge of the cover is aligned with the fold on the exterior. Pin in place to keep the lining under the fold.

18 Sew very close to the fold on exterior.

19 Thread one cord through casing, using a safety pin attached to one end to pull it through the casing easily. Remove safety pin and knot ends. Repeat with second cord from the opposite casing opening.

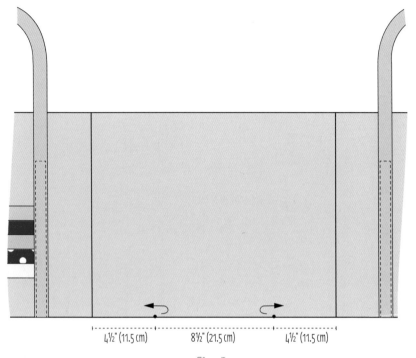

4½" (11.5 cm)   8½" (21.5 cm)   4½" (11.5 cm)

fig. 1

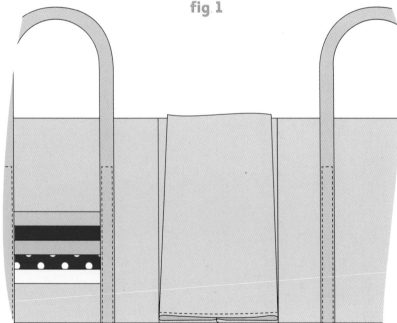

fig. 2

materials

Assorted cotton print scraps, each at least 3" × 4" (7.5 × 10 cm), to make 32 triangle pieces

Cotton print
○ Two 2½" × 14" (6.5 × 35.5 cm) rectangles for top panel

Cotton print
○ Two 4" × 3" (10 × 7.5 cm) rectangles for side panels

Cotton print
○ One 3½" × 7½" (9 × 19 cm) rectangle for base

Cotton print
○ One 12½" × 7½" (31.5 × 19 cm) rectangle for main lining
○ Two 1¾" × 12½" (4.5 × 31.5 cm) rectangles for top panel lining
○ Two 2½" × 3½" (6.5 × 9 cm) rectangles for side panel lining

Lightweight muslin
○ One 14½" × 9½" (37 × 24 cm) rectangle for main panel backing

Medium-weight fusible polyester batting
○ One 14½" × 9½" (37 × 24 cm) rectangle for main pouch
○ Two 2½" × 14" (6.5 × 35.5 cm) rectangles for top panel
○ Two 4" × 3" (10 × 7.5 cm) rectangles for base panel

One 14" (35.5 cm) or longer zipper

One sheet of 8½" × 11" (21.5 × 28 cm) copy paper *(optional)*

Two 2" (5 cm) long twill tapes *(optional)*

tools

Basic Quilting Tools (page 11)

Ruler and pencil

Zipper foot

Quilting adhesive spray

note

All seam allowances are ½" (1.3 cm), unless otherwise indicated.

Triangle Patchwork Box Pouch

Turn your fabric scraps into a box pouch. One of these (the orange one) is made with randomly chosen contrasting fabrics. The other showcases a patchwork of matching colors: pink fabric is matched with white fabric with a pink pattern. Have fun coming up with your own unique patchwork arrangement!

difficulty: ★★★

finished size: 4½" H × 7" W × 3" D (11.5 × 18 × 7.5 cm)

assemble main panel

1 Place fabric scraps on a flat surface and arrange until you are satisfied with the layout.

2 Piece fabric scraps in the method you prefer. You may prefer a standard way of piecing (cutting out triangles and piecing one by one) or a paper-piecing method (page 19—my preferred method). Templates for both methods are provided (figs. 1–2). If you choose paper-piecing, you'll need four of the rectangle templates. You can either photocopy onto paper for foundation piecing or draw the lines on the fabric using a ruler and a pencil.

3 Complete a total of four rows of patchwork; two rows for each side. Sew to connect the two, so

that you have two patchwork panels, each consisting of 16 triangles. Press. Each panel should measure 5" × 7½" (12.5 × 19 cm). Foundation paper can remain on the back of patchwork to stabilize it.

4 Align one of the long edges of the base panel with the bottom edge of one of the patchwork panels, right sides together. Sew close to the edge. Now sew the other long edge of the base panel to the bottom edge of the second patchwork panel. The patchwork panels are now connected, with the bottom panel in between.

5 Apply adhesive spray thoroughly onto nonfusible side of the batting, and place main muslin panel backing on top of it. Smooth to ensure it's well attached.

6 Stitch in the ditch on the seams connecting the base panel to patchwork panels. This will help to shape the box.

7 Quilt around inside of lower triangles on each block close to all edges. The three-piece panel should measure 7½" × 12½" (19 × 31.5 cm). Using a marking pencil, mark the center points on both long edges of this panel 1¼" [2.5 cm] from either corner. Set aside.

assemble top and side panels

8 The top panel with side panels must measure 3½" × 16½" (9 × 42 cm). To ensure that your panel comes out to be this size, this instruction calls for making a larger panel, which you'll trim to size if necessary.

9 Fuse batting to the wrong side of one of the long pieces of the top panel. Sew the long edge of the

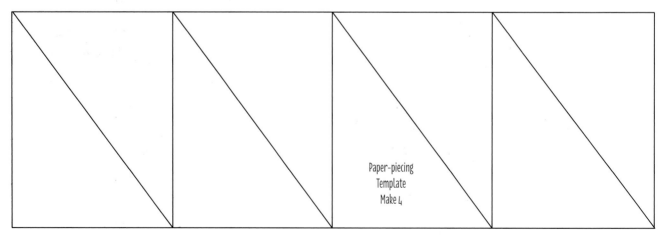

Paper-piecing
Template
Make 4

fig. 1 Template is actual size

top panel to one long edge of the zipper, right sides together. Make sure that the zipper pull remains free from stitching.

10 With the right side of the panel facing up, fold the seam so that the sewn long edge is underneath the panel. Topstitch along the seam. Repeat the same process to attach the second top panel to the other side of the zipper.

11 Trim this top to 12½" (31.5 cm) long. Make sure that the zipper pull is within the center portion before cutting, to avoid damaging your rotary cutter or scissors.

12 Handsew the open zipper end closed. If desired, machine-baste a folded twill tape or something similar at the ends of the zipper, so that its raw edges align with the end of the zipper.

13 Fuse wrong sides of side panels to batting. Align one long edge of one side panel with one short end of the top (zipper) panel. (Don't worry about the widths not matching.) Stitch to join the top piece and the side panel. After these two pieces are joined, topstitch to secure. Attach the second side panel to the top panel.

14 Mark the zipper midpart using a ruler and marker [6" (15 cm) from one side] (fig. 3). From this mark, measure to 8¼" (21 cm) and trim excess. Repeat for the other side of the panel. Trim the width of the entire panel to 3½" (9 cm). Your top panel plus side panels should measure 16½" × 3½" (42 × 9 cm). Mark the center point in both short edges of it (fig. 4).

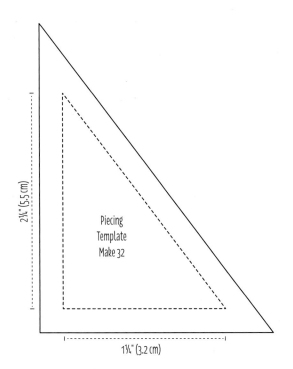

Piecing Template Make 32

2¼" (5.5 cm)

1¼" (3.2 cm)

fig. 2 Template is actual size

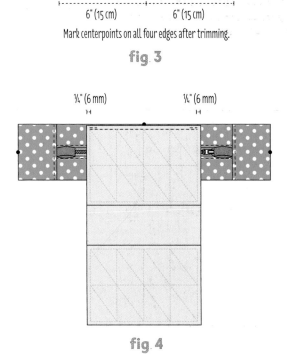

8¼" (21 cm)   8¼" (21 cm)

6" (15 cm)   6" (15 cm)

Mark centerpoints on all four edges after trimming.

fig. 3

¼" (6 mm)   ¼" (6 mm)

fig. 4

assemble pouch exterior

15 Sew one edge at a time. Match the mark on the top panel's long edge with the midpoint of the top edge of the main panel. (This is where the second and the third patchwork rectangles meet.) Pin in place and sew together (**fig. 5**). Make sure to leave ¼" (6 mm) unsewn at both corners. Remember to backstitch at the beginning and the end.

16 Clip into the seam allowance of the top panel a scant ¼" (6 mm), to make it easier to align the top panel with the side edge of the main panel. Clipping like this wherever a straight panel must make a corner makes the process a lot easier. Sew the next edge to the panel, once again leaving a ¼" (6 mm) margin at both edges. Repeat the same process with the other side of the top panel.

17 Repeat with the other side of the main panel, so that the top and side panels are sewn along all but the bottom edges.

18 With the zipper open all the way, match the marks on the bottom edges and sew along the edges. Your pouch exterior is complete. Set aside.

assemble lining

19 With the wrong sides together, fold the long

¼" (6 mm)

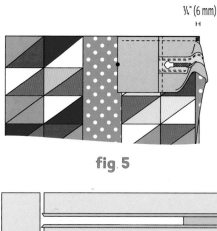

fig. 5

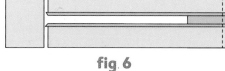

fig. 6

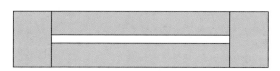

fig. 7

¼" (6 mm)

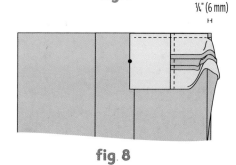

fig. 8

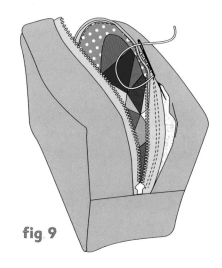

fig. 9

rectangle pieces for top lining panel ¼" (6 mm) at one long edge. Press. With right sides together, place a short edge of these at a long edge of the side lining panel and sew along the edge. Repeat the same process for the other short edge of the top panel lining (figs. 6 and 7).

20 Make the pouch lining the same way you created the pouch exterior in Steps 4–6 (fig. 8). (Remember to mark and clip.)

21 Once your pouch lining is complete, turn it right side out and place the pouch exterior inside the pouch lining. Pin the lining into place, starting with the zipper ends, making sure the lining is closely aligned with the zipper ends. The zipper should be open. Handstitch the lining to the zipper. To make it easier to catch only the zipper while you are handsewing, you can sew just outside the stitching on the zipper (fig. 9).

22 Turn the pouch exterior inside out through the opening.

materials

Neutral cotton solid
- ◯ Two 2¾" × 1¼" (7 × 3.2 cm) rectangles (A, C)
- ◯ One 2¾" × 2" (7 × 5 cm) rectangle (B)
- ◯ Two 1⅛" × 8¼" (2.8 × 21 cm) rectangles (D, E)
- ◯ Two 2" × 1" (5 × 2.5 cm) rectangles for zipper tabs
- ◯ One 3⅝" × 8¼" (9 × 21 cm) rectangle for back exterior

Five assorted cotton prints
- ◯ Five 1" × 4" (2.5 × 10 cm) rectangles (each a different print) for pencil bodies *(left)*
- ◯ Five 1⅛" × 1" (2.8 × 2.5 cm) rectangles (matching print of pencil bodies) for pencil bodies *(right)*

Five assorted cotton solids
- ◯ Five matching cotton solid scraps, each at least 1" × 1" (2.5 × 2.5 cm), for pencil tips
- ◯ Five light beige cotton solid scraps, each at least 1" × 1" (2.5 × 2.5 cm), for pencil wood part
- ◯ Ten light gray cotton solid scraps, each at least 1½" × 1" (3.8 × 2.5 cm), forbackground of pencil tips

Cotton print
- ◯ Two 3⅝" × 8¼" (9 × 21 cm) rectangles for lining

Fusible batting
- ◯ Two 7½" × 3½" (19 × 9 cm) rectangles

One 7" (18 cm) standard zipper (single- or double-pull)

One 1½" (3.8) long ribbon *(optional)*

Embroidery floss *(optional)*

tools

Basic Quilting Tools (page 11)

Fabric glue

One sheet of 8½" × 11" (21.5 × 28 cm) copy paper

note

All seam allowances are ¼" (6 mm), unless otherwise indicated.

Vintage Pencil Case

Inspired by a vintage colored-pencil package, this pencil case features a whimsical patchwork on its exterior. Pick out five of your favorite cotton prints from your stash, together with matching solids. You'll have a lot of fun turning your fabrics into colored pencils! Don't be scared of the stitching on the pencil tips! By the time you are done sewing them, you'll have mastered teeny, tiny piecing and know that it is not nearly as hard as it looks!

difficulty: ★ ★ ★

finished size: 7½" × 3½" (19 × 9 cm)

assemble front exterior

1 Lay five long cotton print rectangles for colored pencils on a flat surface, and choose the arrangement you prefer. Starting with the two rectangles to be placed at the top, sew all five rectangles together, one by one. The resulting panel will measure 2¾" × 4" (7 × 10 cm). (Use a paper-piecing technique for a perfect result. See page 19.) Press seams to one side. Set aside.

2 Paper-piece each of five pencil tips by using five paper photocopies of the tips as a foundation.

3 Sew together one light beige scrap (1) and one solid-colored scrap (2) along one edge with a ¼" (6 mm) seam. Trim to a ⅛" (3 mm) seam allowance and press seam toward beige fabric. On the wrong side of this piece, dab a little bit of fabric glue and attach it to the wrong side of the printed pattern (**fig. 1**). Make sure that the seam will match the line between the pencil tip and wooden part of the pencil. It is very helpful to use sunlight or bright light to see through the paper.

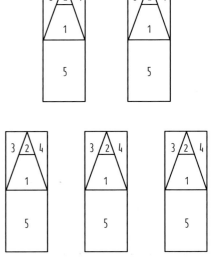

fig. 1 Templates are actual size

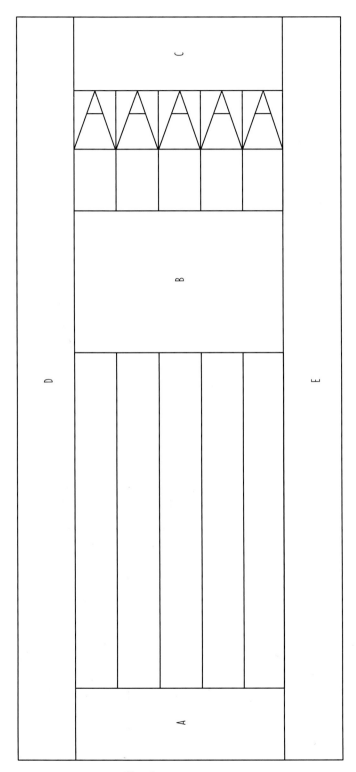

4 Place one solid gray piece (3) onto the right side of the patchwork panel. Turn it to the wrong side and sew along the line between pieces 1 and 2 on the paper. Trim the seam allowance to ⅛" (3 mm), and press to bring the gray solid next to the pencil tip. Repeat the same process to add a gray piece (4) to the other side of the pencil tip. Next, sew the cotton print whose color matches the pencil tip solid (5) to the bottom of the light beige. Use a ruler and a rotary cutter to cut precisely along the four edges. This piece [¹⁵⁄₁₆" × 1¾" (24 mm × 4.5 cm)] has a ¼" (6 mm) seam allowance.

5 Repeat the same process to create a total of five paper-pieced pencil tops and sew these together in the same order as Step 1 to create a patchwork panel that will be on the right window on the pencil case. Set aside.

6 Complete the front exterior rectangle, following the piecing order in **fig. 2**: A – left window – B – right window – C – D – E.

7 Place a fusible batting rectangle fusible side down onto the back of the pieced panel. Center the batting so that the ¼" (6 mm) seam allowance is visible on all sides. Fuse batting to back side of patchwork panel.

8 Edgestitch closely around the two windows with a thread that matches the color of the linen. Use decorative running stitch with embroidery floss to handstitch around the two windows if desired.

assemble back exterior

9 Place the second rectangle of fusible batting fusible side down against the wrong side of the back exterior piece. Center the batting so that a ¼" (6 mm) seam allowance is visible on all sides. Fuse batting to wrong side of back exterior piece.

10 Using thread to match linen, quilt back exterior piece to batting by sewing parallel to long edges, ½" (1.3 cm) apart (see photo on page 119).

assemble pen case

11 Fold each of the two linen zipper tab pieces in half widthwise, wrong sides together, and press.

12 Open one of the zipper tab pieces and place the fold about ¼" (6 mm) to the inside of the zipper stop. Sew along the folded line. Cut off the zipper end (including zipper stop), leaving a narrow seam allowance. Fold back the linen piece and topstitch the folded edge. Repeat on the other short edge of the zipper with the other zipper tab piece.

13 Using a zipper foot, sew together the top long edge of one lining piece and one long edge of the zipper with the right side of the linen and the wrong side of the zipper panel using a seam allowance a bit less than ¼" (6 mm).

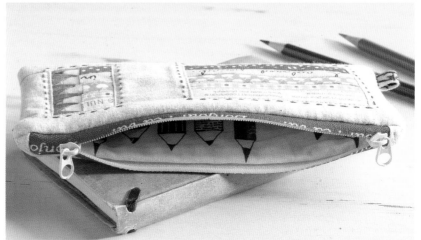

14 Sew the top edge of the front exterior piece to one long edge of the zipper panel, with right sides together. Repeat with the back exterior piece and the other long edge of the zipper panel.

15 If desired, place a folded decorative ribbon on the right side of the front piece close to the corner on the left, raw edges together. Stitch along edge to baste into place.

16 Place right sides of exterior pieces together and pin in place. Repeat for the lining. Sew all edges, leaving approximately 2" (5 cm) opening at the bottom edge of the lining. Turn the right sides out from the opening and handstitch to close.

materials

Cotton print
- ○ One 20" × 14" (51 × 35.5 cm) rectangle for exterior cover

Cotton print
- ○ One 20" × 14" (51 × 35.5 cm) rectangle for interior cover
- ○ One 4" × 6½" (10 × 16.5 cm) rectangle for closure flap

Cotton print
- ○ One fat quarter for binding tape and pocket flap

Cotton solid
- ○ One 14" × 10½" (35.5 × 26.5 cm) rectangle for iPad sleeve
- ○ One 9" × 11" (23 × 28 cm) rectangle for pocket

Cotton flannel
- ○ One 14" × 10½" (35.5 × 26.5) rectangle

Fusible fleece batting
- ○ One 20" × 14" (51 × 35.5 cm) rectangle for cover
- ○ One 14" × 10½" (35.5 × 26.5 cm) rectangle for iPad sleeve
- ○ One 3¼" × 2¾" (8.5 × 7 cm) rectangle for closure flap

Lightweight fusible interfacing
- ○ One 5½" × 5½" (14 × 14) square for sleeve
- ○ One pocket flap

Set of 2" (5 cm) long hook and loop tape pieces

Single snap set

tools

Basic Quilting Tools (page 11)

Quilting guide *(optional)*

I-Love-My-iPad Quilted Cover

This padded cover will protect your iPad nicely. There is a handy pocket for goodies to go along with your iPad, such as a charger, microphones, and cell phone. The sleeve for the iPad is lined with flannel to prevent the screen from being scratched or smudged.

difficulty: ★ ★

finished size: 11¾" × 18" (30 × 45.5 cm) (open)/9" (23 cm) (closed)

assemble cover

1 Sandwich fusible fleece batting between cotton print rectangles for exterior and interior, with fabric wrong sides facing the batting: fuse.

2 Quilt as you like (I quilted diagonally with a 1" [2.5 cm] interval between lines). A quilting guide is a great help to ensure that you are quilting exactly 1" (2.5 cm) away from your previously quilted line.

3 Trim the quilted layers to 18" × 11¾" (45.5 × 30 cm). Sew the middle (9" [23 cm] from both sides) all the way from top to bottom, and back up bottom to top so that there are two rows of stitching. This will make it easier to fold the cover.

4 Sew one piece of hook and loop tape on the exterior, centered from top to bottom with the right long edge of the hook and loop tape ¾" (2 cm) away from the right short edge of the exterior cover. Set aside.

fig. 1
Template is actual size

Fold

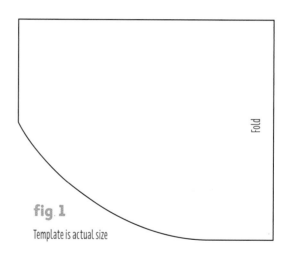

5 Make a quilted iPad sleeve in the same manner you quilted the cover: it will measure 8½" × 11¾" (21.5 × 30 cm).

6 Make a double binding tape to bind the left edge of the quilted sleeve (see page 27). Cut out one 13" × 3" (33 × 7.5 cm) strip from the cotton print for binding tape, fold it in half lengthwise, and press.

7 Sew the binding tape onto the left long edge of the sleeve (with the flannel side down). Handstitch to complete attaching the tape on the back.

8 Place this sleeve panel on the interior cover, flannel side down, with left edges aligned. Pin in place and sew the top, left, and bottom edges of the pocket to the cover using a narrow seam allowance (less than ⅜" [1 cm]). Set aside.

aligned. Topstitch the short pocket edges to the right side of the interior cover, centered between the vertical middle stitched line and the raw edge of the cover, with its bottom raw edge aligned with the bottom edge of the cover. Attach one half of the snap near the top edge of the pocket, as per the instructions that came with the snap.

12 Cut out two 6½" × 3" (16.5 × 7.5 cm) rectangles from the print used for binding for the pocket flap. On the wrong side of one of the pieces, fuse the lightweight interfacing that you cut out using the template provided (fig. 1). With right sides facing, pin these two print pieces together. Sew along the lightweight interfacing, being careful not to sew on top of the interfacing. Leave a 1½" (3.8 cm) wide opening at the straight line (the top edge), and turn the piece right side out from the opening. Press. Attach the other half of the snap in the middle.

13 Attach the two pieces by closing the snap to see where the top edge of the pocket flap will be. Pin the pocket flap to the interior cover and sew very close to the top edge, backstitching ¼" (6 mm) at beginning and end.

14 Make a binding tape in the same manner you made one for the iPad sleeve. This time, you want your binding tape to be at least 32" (81.5 cm) long. I made my binding tape by cutting out four 3" × 18" (7.5 × 45.5 cm) rectangles and sewing short edges diagonally to create one long tape.

15 Sew the tape around all edges of the cover. Handstitch to bring the folded edge to the interior cover.

9 Make a closure flap. Fold the print rectangle for a closure flap in half widthwise and unfold. Place the remaining piece of hook and loop tape in the middle where its right long edge is ⅜" (1 cm) from the folded line you just created and stitch in place.

10 Fold this piece in half widthwise, with right sides together, and sew the long sides' raw edges together. Clip curves. Turn right side out through the opening and insert the batting piece into the pocket, so that there is approximately ¾" (2 cm) near the raw edge with no batting. Press to fuse. Topstitch all edges except for the short raw edge. Position this raw edge on top of the cover exterior in the middle of the left edge, raw

edges together and hook and loop tape side facing out. Sew close to the edge to baste the closure flap and set aside.

11 Fold a solid rectangle for the pocket in half widthwise, with right sides together. Sew together the two side edges. Fuse a lightweight interfacing in the middle of this piece. Clip curves. Turn the piece right side out from the opening and press. Fold along one of the side edges of the interfacing inside the pocket, with pocket interior sides together, and topstitch the edge. Repeat the same process for the other side edge. Fold the short pocket side edges in half lengthwise between the stitched fold and short pocket edges, so that the stitched fold and the short pocket edges are

materials

Cotton print
- ○ Two 13" × 13" (33 × 33 cm) squares for exterior

Cotton print
- ○ Two 9¼" × 13" (23.5 × 33 cm) rectangles for large pocket exteriors

Cotton solid
- ○ Two 9¼" × 13" (23.5 × 33 cm) rectangles for large pocket interiors

Linen
- ○ One 38" × 8½" (96.5 × 21.5 cm) rectangle for exterior

Cotton print
- ○ Two 13" × 13" (33 × 33 cm) squares for interior
- ○ One 38" × 8½" (96.5 × 21.5 cm) rectangle for interior
- ○ One 4½" × 5½" (11.5 × 14 cm) piece for small pocket

Cotton print
- ○ One 6½" × 5½" (16.5 × 14 cm) piece for small pocket

Cotton print
- ○ Two 26" × 10" (66 × 25.5 cm) strips for handles

Materials continued on next page.

Handy Market Tote

This market tote bag, with two large exterior pockets, is roomy enough for your regular grocery shopping trips. It is also a versatile, quick-to-sew gift for family and friends who like to carry a lot of things: books, crafting tools and materials, or even a change of clothing for a yoga class.

difficulty: ★ ★

finished size: 12½" W (bottom) × 20.5" W (top) × 8" D × 12½" H (31.5 × 51 × 20.5 cm × 31.5 cm) [Each strap is approximately 25½" (65 cm) long.]

Medium to heavyweight fusible interfacing*

○ Two 12⅜" × 8⅝" (31.25 × 21.75 cm) rectangles for large pockets

○ Two 12⅜" × 12⅜" (31.25 × 31.25 cm) rectangles for exterior

○ One 37⅜" × 7⅞" (94.75 × 19.75 cm) rectangle for exterior

○ Two 26" × 2⅜" (66 × 5.75 cm) strips for handles

Two 15 mm fabric-covered buttons

Two 2¼" (5.5 cm) long elastic cords

* I usually cut my interfacing a little (⅛" or 3 mm) smaller than the finished size. For this bag, I didn't make the length of interfacing for handles smaller so that I could securely attach the handles by sewing through the interfacing.

tools

Basic Quilting Tools (page 11)

note

All seam allowances are ¼" (6 mm), unless otherwise indicated.

assemble tote exterior

1 Mark the center of the top edge of one of the rectangles for a large pocket. (You may instead lightly fold the fabric piece widthwise to create a crease at the top edge.) With the right side up, place a folded strip so that the short edges are aligned with the center part of the top edge of the rectangle. Machine-baste it using a ⅜" (1 cm) seam allowance.

2 Place one of the solid rectangles on top, right sides together, and sew along the top edge. Press open seam. Carefully fuse interfacing for exterior large pocket on its wrong side. The interfacing should be positioned right under seam allowance; there should be at least a ¼" (6 mm) wide margin on the other three edges of the exterior large pocket where the interfacing is not covered.

3 Fold the piece in half along the seam in the middle with wrong sides together.

4 Fuse interfacing in the center of the wrong side of one of print squares for the bag exterior. Place the pocket piece in Step 3 on its right side, with the bottom edges aligned. Machine-baste the pocket onto the exterior by sewing all edges except for the top edge of the pocket. At the bottom edge on the wrong side, mark the midpoint. Handsew a fabric-covered button centered above the pocket. Repeat the same process to make a second exterior piece with a large pocket.

one long edge of the linen piece is completely sewn to the exterior piece. Repeat the same process with the remaining exterior piece so that it will be attached to the other long edge of the linen. Turn right side out. Set aside.

assemble tote interior

7 Align the top 5½" (14 cm) wide edge of both small pocket pieces and sew along the edge, right sides together. Make a loop to align bottom edges and sew along this edge as well, right sides together. Press open seams. Press the piece, making an approximately ½" (1.3 cm) high border at both top and bottom edges on front. With right sides together, sew along the remaining side edges. Leave an approximately 1½" (3.8 cm) wide opening at one of the side edges, and turn the piece right side out through the opening. Press.

8 Place this pocket piece on the right side of one of the interior squares. Position it 2½" (6.5 cm) from the top edge of the interior top edge, and right in the middle [4" (10 cm)] from one of the side edges. Sew the pocket by stitching very close to all edges except for the top edge of the pocket. Make sure to stitch a little triangle at the top of each side edge to reinforce the pocket attachment.

9 Construct the lining using the same method used to assemble the exterior. Leave an approximately

5 Fuse interfacing onto the middle of the linen rectangle. At both long edges, mark the midpoint on its right side. Take one of the pieces from Step 4 and, right sides together, match the marks. Then sew along the bottom edge, leaving ¼" (6 mm) open at each end. On the linen piece, clip ¼" (6 mm) where the

seam starts and ends, to make the next step easier.

6 Lightly fold the linen piece enough to align its long edge with one of the side edges of the exterior piece. Sew along the edge, right sides together. Do the same with the other side edge so that

10" (25.5 cm) wide opening at the bottom.

make handles and finish tote

10 Fold one of the long pieces for the handles in half lengthwise, wrong sides together. Press, unfold, and bring both long edges to the crease you just made and fold, press, unfold. Fuse interfacing right along the crease closest to one long edge. One long edge of the interfacing strip is very close to the long raw edge of the fabric, while the other long edge is aligned with the crease closest to the edge. Fold the fabric again so that the piece is approximately 2½" (6.5 cm) wide. Topstitch both long edges.

11 Lightly fold the handle in half widthwise to create a center line. Measure and mark 3" (7.5 cm) on either side of the center line. Using the two marks you just created, fold the handle lengthwise toward each mark. Sew a rectangle between the two marks. Repeat the same process to create a second handle.

12 Align the short edges of one handle with the top edge of the bag exterior. Position the handle so that each short end is placed approximately 1" (2.5 cm) to either side of the side edges of the exterior square. Machine-baste. Do the same for the other handle on the other side of the bag exterior.

13 Place the bag exterior inside the lining, right sides together. Sew all the way across the top edge. Turn the bag exterior inside out through the opening on the bottom of the lining. Handstitch opening to close.

14 Topstitch around the top edge to finish.

Wheat Quick Bread

heat flour   1/4c dry milk powder

for Crafting

materials

Assorted cotton print and solid scraps for cover *[2¾" × 2¾" (7 × 7 cm) minimum size]*
○ Sixteen solid
○ Twenty-four print with white background
○ Nine print with yellow background
○ Seven print with other background color

Cotton solid
○ One 9½" × 9½" (24 × 24 cm) square for back cover
○ One fat quarter for a double-fold binding tape

Cotton print
○ One 9½" × 18½" (24 × 47 cm) rectangle for lining base
○ One 9½" × 7½" (24 × 19 cm) rectangle for large pocket
○ One 9½" × 6" (24 × 15 cm) rectangle for small pocket
○ Two 14" × 1½" (35.5 × 3.8 cm) strips for a binding tape

Cotton print
○ One 9½" × 8" (24 × 20.5 cm) rectangle for large pocket back
○ One 9½" × 6½" (24 × 16.5 cm) rectangle for small pocket back

Cotton print
○ Two 8¾" × 2¾" (22 × 7 cm) rectangles for pocket flap

Felt
○ Two 2¾" × 8" (7 × 20.5 cm) rectangles for needle book

Materials continued on next page.

Sweet Trips Embroidery Pouch

This is a great gift for a friend who loves to carry her embroidery items with her when she's on the move. This pouch has a spot for everything she'll need: an embroidery hoop [7" (18 cm) or smaller], small scissors, needles, embroidery floss, and even some fabric and iron-on transfer paper, etc. The vinyl pocket allows your friend to spot the items she needs right away! Use up your scrappy fabrics to make a fun patchwork cover for it.

difficulty: ★★★

finished size: 9½" × 18½" (24 × 47 cm) (open), 9¼" (23.5 cm) square (closed)

Clear vinyl sheet
○ One 8" × 4½" (20.5 × 11.5 cm) rectangle for clear pocket

Lightweight fusible interfacing
○ One 8½" × 3" (21.5 × 7.5 cm) rectangle for pocket flap

Cotton batting
○ One 11½" × 20½" (29 × 52 cm) rectangle

One 18mm wide fabric-covered button (or a button of your choice)*

Tip: If you fuse a piece of lightweight interfacing to the back of your button fabrics prior to covering, it will prevent the metal from shining through the finished button.

One 4½"-long (11.5 cm) elastic cord

One 1½"-long (3.8 cm) ribbon for decoration on pocket flap (optional)

Cotton print for appliqué on back cover (optional)

Fusible web for appliqué (optional)

8½" × 11" (21.5 × 28 cm) copy paper (optional)

Washi or painter's tape (optional)

tools

Basic Quilting Tools (page 11)

Tracing paper (optional)

Pinking shears (optional)

Quilting adhesive spray

note

All seam allowances are ¼" (6 mm), unless otherwise indicated.

assemble patchwork cover

1 Using templates (fig. 1), cut out pieces from assorted print and solid scraps. To avoid confusion, have a colored sketch next to you as you put together the fabric pieces. Divide the patchwork into square and rectangular sections, in order to work on one shape at a time. [I divided it into 13 sections: 9 squares in the middle and 4 borders (2 long top and bottom borders and 2 short side borders).] If you prefer paper-piecing, draw templates on copy paper to make 13 templates, divided as described above. (See paper-piecing on page 19.)

2 Once the patchwork cover is all pieced, place the solid fabric for a back cover on the patchwork piece, right sides together, and sew along the left edge. Press seam open. If desired, appliqué some fabric on the back cover using fusible web. (See raw-edged appliqué on page 27.)

{ tip }
To ensure straight stitching, use washi or painter's tape, which can be attached right next to stitching and can be removed very easily.

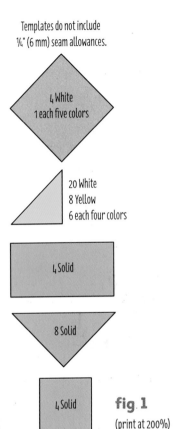

Templates do not include ¼" (6 mm) seam allowances.

4 White
1 each five colors

20 White
8 Yellow
6 each four colors

4 Solid

8 Solid

4 Solid

fig. 1
(print at 200%)

3 Apply adhesive spray thoroughly on the wrong side of the cover and attach it to cotton batting. [Cotton batting should be approximately 1" (2.5 cm) larger than the cover around all edges.]

4 Quilt as desired. I machine-stitched, outlining all white pieces with white thread and outlining around all stars using aqua green thread to match the border color. If you have an appliqué, quilt around its edges using zigzag machine-stitching or handstitching. Once quilting is completed, trim batting flush with fabric edges to 9½" × 18½" (24 × 47 cm).

5 Handsew a fabric-covered button in the middle of the piecework front panel 1" (2.5 cm) from the right edge. At the left edge, machine-baste cording in the middle, so that the ends align and meet at the left edge. (Use a narrow seam allowance.)

assemble lining

6 Align top edges of the two small pocket pieces, with right sides facing, and sew together. Press seam toward longer piece. With the longer piece toward the back, wrong sides together, align the bottom edges of the pieces and press again. There should be approximately a ¼" (6 mm) border created at the top edge due to the fabric for the pocket back being a little longer than the front piece. Sew very close to the bottom edge of the border, with a front side up. Repeat the same process with fabric pieces for the larger pocket.

7 Place these pockets (small one on top of large one) on the lining base with left edges aligned. Machine-baste the pockets to lining by sewing top, left, and bottom edges, using a ⅛" (3 mm) seam allowance. Set aside.

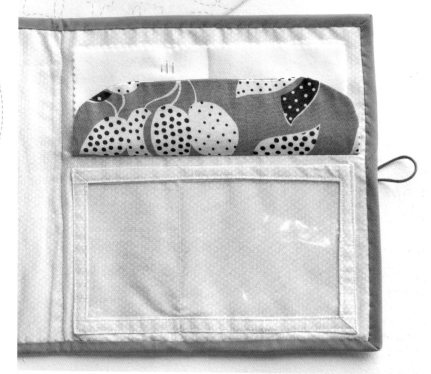

{ tip }

If you are using a vinyl that does not feed easily through your sewing machine's feed dog, attach tracing paper underneath the vinyl to improve traction. After stitching is done, remove tracing paper.

8 Refer to the instructions on making binding (page 27) and make a ⅜" (1 cm) wide binding tape. Bind all around edges of the vinyl sheet. Bring the long folded edge to the back of the vinyl piece and sew along the tape very close to the vinyl part, starting from the top right edge and down to the bottom, then up to the top left edge.

9 Place this vinyl piece on the right side of the lining base. It should be centered on the right half of the lining base. Position it so that the bottom edge of the pocket is approximately ½" (1.3 cm) from the bottom edge of the lining. Sew very close to all edges of the pocket, except for the top edge. Divide the vinyl pocket by stitching in the width desired. I wanted the left portion of the pocket to hold a small pair of scissors, so I made the left part 3" (7.5 cm) wide.

10 Trace a pocket flap pattern (fig. 2) on the nonfusible side of the fusible interfacing and cut. Fuse this interfacing on the wrong side of one of the pocket flap fabric pieces. If desired, machine-baste a folded ribbon along the top edge. [The short edges of it should be just ½" (1.3 cm) above the top edge of the interfacing.] Place this fabric on top of the other fabric for a pocket

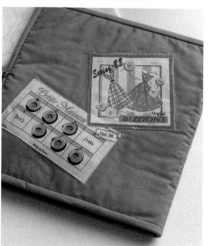

flap, with right sides together. Sew ₁⁄₁₆" (1.5 mm) along the edges of the interfacing. Leave a small opening [1½" (3.8 cm)] at a top edge. Clip corners and trim seam allowances if needed, and turn right side out through the opening. Press. Place this flap just ½" (1.3 cm) above the vinyl pocket and sew very close to the top edge.

11 Pink edges of felt pieces if desired. Center the two felt rectangles above the pocket flap, layering one on top of the other. Sew down the middle through the two layers of felt.

finish pouch

12 With the wrong sides together, place the lining on top of the batting side of the cover. Pin in place and sew through the layers down the middle from top to bottom, along cover seam line. Machine-baste all edges using a ⅛" (3 mm) seam allowance. Make a double-fold binding tape that is 2" (5 cm) wide and at least 60" (152.5 cm) long, using the method described on page 27. Bind all around the edges of the pouch using a ¼" (6 mm) seam allowance. Handstitch to finish attaching the binding.

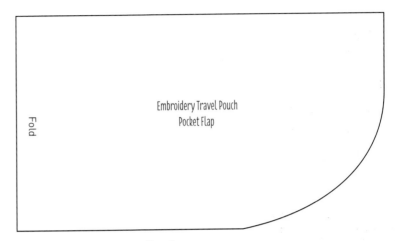

Fold

Embroidery Travel Pouch
Pocket Flap

fig. 2 Template is actual size

materials

Linen
- One 4½" × 4½" (11.5 × 11.5 cm) square for bottom
- Sixteen scraps measuring 2" × 1.5" (5 × 3.8 cm) for top

Assorted cotton prints
- Four 2" × 2¼" (5 × 5.5 cm) pieces for patchwork on top
- Four 1½" × 4½" (3.8 × 11.5 cm) rectangles for sides
- Two 1½" × 1½" (3.8 × 3.8 cm) squares for covering buttons

One sheet of 8.5" × 11" (21.5 × 28 cm) copy paper

Two ¾" (2 cm) wide fabric-covered buttons

Polyfill

tools

Basic Quilting Tools (page 11)

Fabric glue stick

note

All seam allowances are ¼" (6 mm). unless otherwise indicated.

Prettified Pincushion

Pincushions are probably my favorite things to make, because they are great stash-busting projects! This pincushion design showcases four different fabrics on the top and four others on its sides. Grab your pretty fabric scraps and whip these up for friends who are new to sewing!

difficulty: ★★

finished size: 4" W × 1" H × 4" D (10 × 2.5 × 10 cm)

assemble patchwork top

1 Trace the template (fig. 1) provided for paper-piecing and cut. Create four of these paper foundations.

2 Take one of the foundation pieces and dab glue on the wrong side of the paper in the middle; place one cotton scrap underneath the paper with the wrong sides together. Paper-piece linen pieces all around to complete the first panel. Repeat the process for remaining foundations, so that you will have four patchwork panels finished at 2½" × 2½" (6.5 × 6.5 cm).

3 Place panels on a flat surface and arrange into your desired layout. Sew the top two pieces together, with right sides facing, to create a center seam. Press seam to one side. Repeat the same process for the remaining pieces and press seams to the opposite side. Sew the two pieced sections together and press open seams to complete patchwork top.

assemble sides

4 Sew together two of the long print rectangles with right sides facing, using a 1" (2.5 cm) long seam along one short edge and leaving ¼" (6 mm) at both top and bottom. Repeat the same process three more times to create a patchwork loop consisting of four cotton rectangles. Press open seam.

5 One by one, sew each long rectangular side piece to the top patchwork panel. Pin and align one top long edge of one of the four rectangles with one edge of the patchwork panel in Step 3, right sides together. Sew the aligned edge, being very careful not to sew other parts of the side panel. Make sure that you are leaving ¼" (6 mm) unstitched at both ends so that the seam length is 4" (10 cm) long. Remove the pins. Repeat the same process for the remaining long rectangle pieces so that the loop will be completely sewn onto the patchwork top.

6 Sew the raw edge of the loop to the linen bottom piece in the same manner. This time, leave a 1½" (3.8 cm) opening in the middle of one edge.

7 Turn the pincushion right side out through the opening. Fold along the seam between the top and side: press. Do the same for the remaining seven seams to form a sharp shape.

8 Fill the pincushion with polyfill. Using a little bit of polyfill at a time, fill the farthest corners first.

Once the pincushion is nicely firm, handsew the opening to close.

9 Following the manufacturer's instructions, create two fabric-covered buttons. Sew one button onto the center top of the pincushion, then run the needle and thread through the pincushion to the bottom; sew the second button to the bottom center.

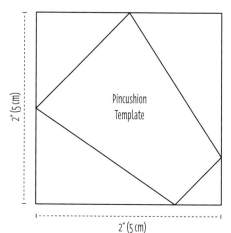

2" (5 cm)

Pincushion Template

2" (5 cm)

fig. 1 Template is actual size

Resources

There are so many wonderful fabric stores these days—from chain stores such as Jo-Ann Fabric and Craft Stores, to great independent stores. You probably already have your favorites. That's why I'm offering just a few suggestions for online fabric buying.

EQUILTER
The best selection of interesting fabrics!

equilter.com

ETSY
Anything crafty can be found in here—the best place to hunt down Japanese fabric and artisan handprinted linen fabric.

etsy.com

HAWTHORNE THREADS
A great selection of modern fabrics.

hawthornethreads.com

FAT QUARTER SHOP
A great selection of nice fat-quarter bundles.

fatquartershop.com

FABRIC.COM
Lots of fabrics at bargain prices.

fabric.com

FABRICS-STORE.COM
Quality linen in a variety of weights and colors.

fabrics-store.com

SEW, MAMA, SEW!
Modern fabrics and lovely blog.

sewmamasew.com

SUPERBUZZY
The best selection of Japanese kawaii and quirky fabrics!

superbuzzy.com

ZIP IT
Quality zippers.

etsy.com/shop/zipit

Index

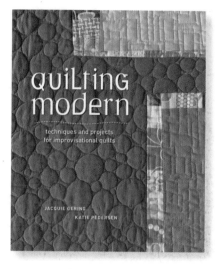